DAILY DEVOTIONS
INSPIRED BY

90 MINUTES
IN HEAVEN

Daily Devotions
Inspired by
90 Minutes
In Heaven

90 READINGS FOR HOPE AND HEALING

Don Piper
and Cecil Murphey

BERKLEY PRAISE, NEW YORK

THE BERKLEY PUBLISHING GROUP
Published by the Penguin Group
Penguin Group (USA) Inc.
375 Hudson Street, New York, New York 10014, USA
Penguin Group (Canada), 90 Eglinton Avenue East, Suite 700, Toronto, Ontario M4P 2Y3, Canada
(a division of Pearson Penguin Canada Inc.)
Penguin Books Ltd., 80 Strand, London WC2R 0RL, England
Penguin Group Ireland, 25 St. Stephen's Green, Dublin 2, Ireland (a division of Penguin Books Ltd.)
Penguin Group (Australia), 250 Camberwell Road, Camberwell, Victoria 3124, Australia
(a division of Pearson Australia Group Pty. Ltd.)
Penguin Books India Pvt. Ltd., 11 Community Centre, Panchsheel Park, New Delhi—110 017, India
Penguin Group (NZ), 67 Apollo Drive, Rosedale, North Shore 0632, New Zealand
(a division of Pearson New Zealand Ltd.)
Penguin Books (South Africa) (Pty.) Ltd., 24 Sturdee Avenue, Rosebank, Johannesburg 2196,
South Africa

Penguin Books Ltd., Registered Offices: 80 Strand, London WC2R 0RL, England

The publisher does not have any control over and does not assume any responsibility for author or third-party
websites or their content.

PRINTING HISTORY
Berkley Praise hardcover edition / November 2006
Berkley Praise trade paperback edition / December 2009

Berkley Praise trade paperback ISBN: 978-0-425-23208-8

The Library of Congress has catalogued the Berkley Praise hardcover edition as follows:

Piper, Don, 1950–
    Daily devotions inspired by 90 minutes in heaven : 90 readings for hope and healing / by
Don Piper and Cecil Murphey.
        p. cm.
    ISBN 0-425-21455-9
    1. Devotional literature.   2. Hope—Religious aspects—Christianity.   I. Murphey, Cecil
B.   II. Title.   III. Title: Daily devotions inspired by ninety minutes in heaven.
    BV4801.P57 2006
    242'.2—dc22   2006022023

PRINTED IN THE UNITED STATES OF AMERICA

10   9   8   7   6   5   4   3   2   1

Scripture identified as
*   are taken from the *Holy Bible*, New Living Translation, copyright © 1996. Used by permission of Tyndale
House Publishers, Inc., Wheaton, Illinois 60189. All rights reserved.
**   are taken from the *Holy Bible*, New International Version. Copyright © 1973, 1978, 1984 International
Bible Society. Used by permission of Zondervan Bible Publishers.
*** are taken from the *Holy Bible*, Today's New International Version TNIV. Copyright © 2001, 2005 by
International Bible Society. Used by permission of International Bible Society. All rights reserved worldwide.
†   are taken from the King James Version of the Bible. Copyright © 1979, 1980, 1982 by Thomas Nelson,
Inc., Publishers.
††   are taken from *The Message*. Copyright © 1993, 1994, 1995, 1996, 2000, 2001, 2002. Used by permission
of NavPress Publishing Group.

ACKNOWLEDGMENTS

Don Piper: When 90 Minutes in Heaven: A True Story of Death and Life *(Fleming Revell) appeared in the fall of 2004, I was reasonably certain that my parents would buy a couple of copies. Some close friends, neighbors, and my church family at First Baptist Church of Pasadena, Texas, could probably be counted on to purchase copies, as well. Frankly, I assumed that the remaining books of the first printing (and presumptively, the only printing) would fill my garage for the rest of my natural life.*

A million copies and thirty printings later have only succeeded in confirming what I have always believed: I do not have the gift of prophecy. My garage is still mainly used for the purpose for which it was designed . . . cars and other stuff I just can't seem to let go of. And my first book is found on bookshelves in virtually every corner of the world. It has been translated in fourteen languages thus far, a large-print edition, and I have recorded an audio version.

But for me, the phenomenal sales success has been eclipsed by the individual responses. Hundreds of thousands of e-mails, phone calls, letters, and face-to-face encounters have been deeply humbling and quite overwhelming. From Stockholm to Honolulu, I have looked into the eyes of many souls longing for hope and healing. Whether in small towns like Salem, Olney, York, and West Plains, or major cities like Portland, Los Angeles, Detroit, and Tampa, the needs and responses are virtually the same.

This book contains many of those dramatic and poignant responses. And you'll find scriptures and prayers to complete each daily devotional thought. It is our desire that these ninety daily devotions will bring the same encouragement, illumination, and hope that so many seemed to take from 90 Minutes in Heaven.

Such a book could not be possible without my gifted writing partner and friend, Cecil Murphey. The importance of what Cec brings to the table cannot be exaggerated.

We are both deeply indebted to our literary agent, Deidre Knight, who believed in this project without reservation. I want to acknowledge my deep gratitude to the fine professionals at Berkley for their confidence in this book, especially Denise Silvestro. My family: sons, Chris and Joe; daughter, Nicole; son-in-law, Scott; and wife, Eva, have been a continual source of unwavering support. As have our parents, Ralph and Billie Piper and Eldon and Ethel Pentecost.

And yet, this book could not exist without the precious souls from New Jersey to San Diego who shared their stories with Cec and me, in quiet moments, often with tears in their eyes. Their stories are the heartbeat of this book. To those dear folks, I offer my thanks. May the Lord encourage you, strengthen you, and give you hope. And to all who read Daily Devotions Inspired by 90 Minutes in Heaven *. . . may you receive courage and have faith for another day. Amen.*

Cec Murphey: *I also want to thank our wonderful agent, Deidre Knight, and Denise Silvestro and the team at Berkley. But most of all, thank God for Shirley.*

Contents

Now faith is being sure of what we hope for and certain of what we do not see.

—HEBREWS 11:1***

1

MINISTER OF HOPE

These days, I am often introduced as the Minister of Hope, and I like that title. I don't take that term lightly or boastfully, because I feel God has called me to bring hope to all and to point the way to heaven.

My story is simple. On January 18, 1989, I died in an automobile accident—and it wasn't a near-death experience. Two EMTs pronounced me dead and I spent ninety minutes in heaven before a pastor prayed me back to earth.

Because of my heavenly experience, I know what awaits us after this life on earth is finished. I've already visited heaven and I've come back to talk about it. Because I was there, I don't have to guess or imagine what heaven will be like. I only have to tell what I saw, felt, and heard. That's why I can offer encouragement and help others prepare for the great experience that lies ahead once we leave this life.

Hope is the most important message I have to offer. In this book, when I use the word *hope*, I mean it in the biblical sense. In the Old Testament, the Hebrew word always implied an expectation of good—never a word of dread or fearful torment. In the New Testament, *elpis* is the most common Greek word translated as hope. In every one of its fifty-four uses, *elpis* conveys certainty and assurance. It's not a wish or a desire; it's a reasonable expectation.

We don't hope for those things that are already present because we see them now. Hope refers to those things we can't see and yet we're positive they exist, and we anticipate seeing them sometime in the future. The words *hope* and *faith* are tied closely together. Hope anticipates, and faith believes. We can't hope unless we believe something better lies ahead.

Along with hope, the New Testament urges us to wait patiently. That means to hold on and to endure because we know the end result. Hope, in the Bible, implies that, because we earnestly look forward to a glorious future, we can endure any sufferings along the way as we wait for what we will one day inherit. It's like the painful experience of a marathon runner—the pace is grueling, but the reward is worth pushing on to the end. Because we have the words of the New Testament to assure us of our eternal hope, we live in joyful anticipation. Then God sends a person like me, who comes along and says, "It's real. I've been there." When I speak publicly, I can see the expectation level rise in the eyes of my listeners.

In this book, I stress hope, because I believe that's the important factor that many people haven't grasped. No matter what the trial, the hardship, the pain, or the suffering, for God's people there is something yet ahead. If we're assured of that fulfillment—if we truly hope—we can face our daily trials and hardships, and God gives us the ability to hold on during the worst of times.

Anticipate the best because it's yet to come. I can say that because I've already seen what's to come.

My Heavenly Father, fill me with hope—true hope—that looks forward to the joyful life ahead when I will live forever in your holy and loving presence. Amen.

*Whom have I in heaven but you? I desire
you more than anything on earth.*
—Psalm 73:25*

2

ALONE AT THE GATE

I was in Florida and a number of people crowded around me
after I preached. This often happened and I gladly signed
books, answered questions, and tried to offer hope and reassurance to all who reached out to me. But there was one woman
who stood at my side for a long time saying nothing. Finally I
turned to her and asked, "Can I help you?"

"I need to talk to you."

Her words alone were not unusual, but the intensity of her
voice made me realize she wanted to talk about something
highly significant to her. "I'll be glad to talk to you," I said and
I invited her to talk while I autographed more books.

"No, I'll wait until everyone's gone," she said.

"I don't know how long that will be."

"I'll wait," she replied and sat in a chair a few feet away. At least half an hour passed before the others left. As soon as we were alone, she scooted her chair over and sat close to me.

"Thank you for allowing me to visit with you," she said before she dropped her head and began to weep.

I have had the pleasure of meeting tens of thousands of people at my speaking events, and I am honored that I have been able to touch their hearts. Many share their pain, their doubts, and their fears, and tears are often shed as they relate their stories.

I patted the young woman's hand and gently asked, "What's troubling you? You're obviously very hurt."

Still looking down, she caught her breath and said, "Last year, I lost Justin, my nine-year-old son. He drowned."

"I'm so sorry for your temporary separation from your son."

She looked up. "Yes, yes, it is temporary, isn't it?"

"You bet it is. Absolutely."

"Justin became a Christian early last year," she said. She gave me a terrible account about a dysfunctional family situation and added, "Justin and I were the only Christians in our family."

"I'm glad Justin had the opportunity to turn to the Lord before he went to be—"

"That's what I wanted to speak to you about. Tonight I heard you talk about heaven and the fact that you were so happy to be there because of the reunion you had with other people who went before you. You felt such great joy being with those other Christians you had known on Earth."

"That's exactly what happened." I started to add, "It was glorious," but the troubled look on her face stopped me.

"Your testimony touched me and it was just wonderful. I can't wait to have a reunion with Justin." She wiped away fresh tears and said, "But I'm also heartbroken."

Confused, I leaned forward and asked if she grieved over Justin's death.

"Of course I do, but it's not that. You see, at the time he drowned, both of us were new believers. Justin didn't know any Christians—not any who have, you know, have died— and . . ." She stopped and burst into tears again.

I still wasn't sure what troubled her so deeply. I waited until she finally told me.

"I'm so concerned that he got to heaven and no one was there to meet him."

I paused and felt her pain, this poor woman imagining her little boy all alone in heaven. But I also knew God doesn't abandon those who love Him. I looked the concerned mother in the eyes and spoke to her words that I knew in my heart were true.

"Justin wasn't alone in heaven."

"You think so?"

"I *know it*. Even if there were no friends or relatives to greet him."

I saw the confusion in her eyes so I patted her hand and

continued, "If there wasn't anybody at the gate to meet him, Jesus came and met him. He wouldn't let Justin stand at the gate by himself."

Her face brightened instantly. "I've been so concerned that he had to be there all alone."

"No one is ever alone," I said. "Never. Not ever."

As she stared at my face, the words sank in. "Yes, I understand that now. Jesus is with him even if there's no one else."

"And if he has Jesus—"

"Yes, that will be enough, won't it?"

"I can't think of anything better."

Lord Jesus, remind me that I'm never alone. Remind me that even when I feel alone, you're with me. You're by my side now; you're already waiting for me in heaven. Thank you, Lord, that I'll never, ever be alone. Amen.

Remember your promise to me, for it is my only hope.
Your promise revives me; it comforts me in all my troubles.

—PSALM 119:49–50*

3

HOPE: A REASON TO LIVE

For me, the saddest word in English is *hopeless*. It means we give up; we stop trying, and we can't or won't put the effort into fighting. I also believe that *hopeless* isn't part of God's vocabulary.

Yet hopelessness seems to abound at certain times. After great tragedies such as hurricanes, tsunamis, or the killing of soldiers in war, the level of hope declines. But it is during times of hardship and suffering that we need hope the most, for when we have an "all-is-lost" attitude we truly are lost.

This truth is vividly illustrated in the classic book *Man's Search for Meaning* by Viktor Frankl. After World War II, Frankl wrote of his experiences in a Nazi concentration camp. One of the things that struck me when I read the book twenty years ago was that between Christmas of 1944 and New Year's Day (the last year of World War II), more prisoners died than at any previous time. Frankl said it wasn't because they worked harder or that their food supplies had been cut, or even because of diseases in the camps. The problem was that all of them heard rumors and knew the end of the war was near. They lived with the expectation that they would be liberated before Christmas. As the days passed and they received no encouraging news that the Allied Forces would be there soon, many prisoners became discouraged. They lost hope. As each man lost hope, he stopped fighting to live, and within days, he died. When one prisoner lost hope, that was bad enough, but one man's dejection infected another and soon that negative, hopeless attitude spread like an epidemic.

What Frankl realized, and what we need to see today, is that we can't stop tragedy from striking, and we can't just tell people, "Stop that! Think positive! Stop whining!" What we have to do is help them find a reason to live, or to focus on a future goal of some kind.

Members of Alcoholics Anonymous understand this principle. They speak of living one day at a time. They teach members to concentrate on living and staying sober today. "Just for today," they say to each other. When an alcoholic survives one full day without a drink, no matter how difficult, it offers hope for the next day. "I did it yesterday. I can do it again today."

The psalmist expressed this same idea: "For you have been

my hope, O Sovereign Lord, my confidence since my youth. From birth I have relied on you . . ." (Psalm 71:5–6a**).

Hope. A reason to live. The French term *raison d'être* means a reason for existing or a justification for living. That's the secret. As long as we have a reason, we can take the next step. And the next. And the next.

God of all hope, forgive me when I become discouraged or want to give up. Deliver me from self-pity and renew my hope. Enable me to see that I can not only make it through the troubles of today, but you give me hope and comfort to make it each day. Amen.

[Jesus said,] "Don't be troubled. You trust God, now trust in me. There are many rooms in my Father's home, and I am going to prepare a place for you."

—John 14:1–2[*]

4

UNIMAGINABLE

An article in *Newsweek* magazine reported on people with Familial Dysautonomia (FD), also known as Riley-Day Syndrome. It's a disease that causes certain nervous systems to malfunction. One symptom is that the sufferers aren't aware of being hurt. They break bones or damage their bodies, but their pain sensors never feel the injury.

I once talked with a young man with FD who had no inkling of what it felt like to feel physical pain. He had suffered a number of broken bones and had recently received eleven stitches in his forehead. He had heard about pain and his friends talked about aches and hurts, he said, but pain was unimaginable to him.

"Unimaginable," I mumbled to myself afterward.

As difficult as pain was for the young man with FD to comprehend, it's also much like that when it comes to our concept of heaven. We read the few references in the Bible about the wonderful life yet ahead, but we don't get it—not really. We know heaven is real, that it's a place of perfect joy and complete happiness. We can say those words, but we can't imagine what lies ahead. We hope and we may yearn for the perfect life, but how can we possibly grasp what it's like?

I know about the wonder and the perfection of heaven because I spent an hour and a half there. I can assure people, and I often do, that there is no sorrow in heaven. Because I've been there, I can still close my eyes and hear beautiful music beyond anything I've ever heard on Earth. In heaven is perfect peace, and the joy is beyond my human words to explain.

Unimaginable. Perhaps that *is* the best word.

I try to describe heaven—and in my heart and head I know what it's like, but others will know it only when they experience it for themselves. In the meantime, whether people listen to me or read the Bible, they can only try to envision what it will be like, and the reality will far exceed their wildest dreams.

The real thing will make everything they've heard about heaven pale in comparison. Years ago, Cec wrote a book about Antarctica with Norman Vaughan, the then last-surviving member of Admiral Richard E. Byrd's historic trip to Antarctica,

1928–1930.[1] Norman's tales about the white continent filled Cec with excitement and made him wish he could have been there. Cec also read books by others about the last continent, including accounts by Byrd himself. Cec did as much research as he could so he could write the book. He read about crevasses, icebergs, skua birds, sea lions, and a land that was white in every direction, but no matter how much information he had, it wasn't the same as being there.

Five years later, Cec wrote a second book with Norman about Antarctica and it stirred his imagination again. In 2004, Cec decided to see the ice-covered continent for himself. He flew to the southern tip of Argentina, boarded a small ship, and sailed for two days in extremely rough water. Because only scientists live on the continent, visitors can land but not stay overnight. On motorized dinghies, the forty-eight passengers made eleven landings from the ship.

"Antarctica was so much greater than anything I had imagined" was his first response. He walked within three feet of penguins and about the same distance from seals. He had seen pictures of the pristine white icebergs with blue hues of encased water, but when he saw them in person he stared at them in awe.

---

[1] *With Byrd at the Bottom of the World: The South Pole Expedition of 1928–1930* by Norman D. Vaughan with Cecil Murphey (Stackpole Books, 1990).

That's what happened when I was in heaven. I had heard and read about heaven's magnificence, but experiencing it myself was something else. No matter how specific and detailed the descriptions, nothing came close to what I witnessed myself.

Many have written books about heaven, but they can only describe what they *think* it will be like. I can describe heaven because I *know* what it's like; yet, no matter how vivid my words, heaven is still beyond human comprehension. Even though I brought back a firsthand report with all the assurances of the overwhelming joy that fills the atmosphere and the hearts of those already there, it's still unimaginable.

That's part of the mystery and the joy of our anticipated future home. Heaven *is* unimaginable, but it's not untrue or impossible. As Jesus said, he has prepared a place for us. We can't know what it will be like, but we can live with the sense that it is real. We can imagine the joy, the peace, the freedom from pain, the deliverance from problems, but we'll never know the experience until we're there.

God of love, help me to remember that you already have a place reserved for me in heaven. Even though I can't imagine how marvelous it will be, enable me to live the rest of my life in anticipation of moving into that eternal home. Amen.

But I trust in you, O Lord; I say, "You are my God."
My times are in your hands . . .
—PSALM 31:14–15A***

5

WHY DID YOU WAIT SO LONG?

"Why did you take so long to write about your trip to heaven and back?" I hear that question quite regularly. During the first few months after we wrote *90 Minutes in Heaven*, I said to audiences, "It took me a long time to become comfortable with sharing such a painful, intimate memory."

That was true. But another reason was that I was afraid people would think I was crazy. Or they would insist I had had only a near-death experience (NDE). Despite the fact that in the book we make a strong statement that it was not an NDE, a couple of the first reviewers either skipped that section or didn't believe me.

It definitely wasn't an NDE. Two EMTs—men who knew their business—pronounced me *dead* and there was no evidence of life for at least ninety minutes. If I had not been truly dead, either I would have bled out and died, or my brain would have been so oxygen deprived that I would have been a total vegetable.

But some people are so skeptical that the evidence and my testimony mean nothing to them. So why would I want to go around telling people my story? Who wants to be disputed or disbelieved? And I certainly didn't want to be labeled a kook. So, I was hesitant to speak up.

But then I realized something: There will always be skeptics and my job isn't to refute them. I have a mission and that is to spread hope to the hurting. I believe I have a divine commission to spread the message of hope wherever I have the chance to speak.

Why God chose me, I have no idea. And to be honest, there wasn't some great moment when God confronted me and commanded me to go out and preach. I began to share my testimony because it seemed like the right thing to do. I did it because I wouldn't be at peace unless I did. I understand Paul's cry to the Corinthians, "Woe to me if I do not preach the gospel!" (1 Corinthians 9:16b**).

When I first began to speak (cautiously) about my trip to heaven, I had no idea how people would respond. To my surprise, they listened. Sometimes they nodded and smiled. But the most common response, and the one that I liked most, was that confused and hurting people found courage to face their ordeals.

I'm proud of being called the Minister of Hope. I can (and do) preach messages on many topics, but hope is what I try to offer. At one point, I wondered if I was doing the right thing by going out and speaking. Was I exploiting an experience? Was I capitalizing on something private?

One thought, however, kept coming to me. If I had a gallon of water and people around me were thirsty, would it be right for me to withhold it?

I've come to realize that God prepared me to bring assurance and peace to hurting hearts. Instead of telling why I waited so long, I think I need to say, "I started to speak publicly at exactly the right time." You see, although I knew that my ninety minutes in heaven was a great gift from God, I needed to realize it was a gift I had to share. I needed to understand that by speaking about my experience I could give a gift to others—a gift of hope.

My story is more dramatic than most, but many others have had experiences when they felt they would never make it, when life became so overwhelming they were sure they would fail totally or die. But then they overcame their obstacles, triumphed over their tragedies, and as they share their experiences, they too offer hope. That's one of the things we can do for each other: We can hold out hope and the promise of a better future to those who feel alone and discouraged.

Maybe the greatest gift we can offer others in their low moments is what I try to offer every time I speak: God knows your situation and God cares. That is the message of hope I offer.

Holy God, sometimes I feel alone, deserted, rejected, and hopeless. Speak to me. Send your messengers with words of hope. Send those who bring me the words of encouragement, the gentle touches, and the loving embraces—because I need them. And, God, as you lift me from my low places, use my life and my experience to bring hope to others. Amen.

You chart the path ahead of me . . .
Every moment you know where I am.
—PSALM 139:3*

6
A SOLDIER IN IRAQ

He was on active duty in Baghdad a few months after the invasion of Iraq. While on guard duty, a car bomb exploded a few feet away from him. Although another guard died instantly, the twenty-one-year-old soldier survived the bomb; however, he was so critically injured the medics correctly assessed that they couldn't transfer him to a hospital.

On a stretcher, they carried the young soldier into a field hospital to make him comfortable. "It's just a matter of time," one corpsman whispered to another.

A nurse at the field hospital came to the patient. She knew he would die within the next few hours and wanted to find some way to comfort him in his last moments. In her hands, she held a copy of *90 Minutes in Heaven*. "May I read something to you?" she asked.

The soldier, conscious enough to understand what was going on, nodded.

She sat beside the young man and read about my experiences after I died and went to heaven. She paused once to make sure he was still alert enough to understand.

"Don't stop," he said weakly. "Keep reading."

A few minutes later, he shut his eyes and she started to close the book.

"Please," he whispered in a strained voice, "I want to hear the rest. It makes me feel better."

She continued to read. Seconds after she read the part where I was prayed back to earth, the soldier died. "He had a peaceful look on his face," the nurse said. "I know he understood. He was also ready and I believe the words prepared him for what lay ahead."

I learned the story of the young solider because the boy's mother came to one of my book signings. "The nurse wrote to the family and told us what happened," she said. "You have no idea what those words meant to me."

I stopped signing books and focused on her. It was one of the most powerful testimonies I had heard and I was deeply touched.

"Our son was a believer, so we never worried about where he would go after he died." She wiped away tears before she added, "We found great comfort in knowing that his last thoughts were about his new home. In those final moments, he prepared himself for what lay ahead." She grabbed me and hugged me. "And I wanted to thank you for telling your story because it came at exactly the right time for our son."

I held her while tears coursed down her face. "I have such deep peace now," she said. "If I had to lose my son, the ending could not have been more beautiful. He was ready to go and you gave him a preview of his new life."

I never saw the woman again and I can't remember her name, but it was one of those special moments for me. I felt as if God had used me—thousands of miles away—to minister to dying disciples. That incident took place at one of those times when my body was exhausted from days of nonstop travel and I felt mentally wiped out. When I first began to sign books that day, I thought, "I wish I hadn't agreed to do this."

After the mother left, I silently asked God to forgive me for such an attitude. Fresh energy pumped into my body as I realized God had used my life and my efforts to bring comfort to a dying man at an isolated field hospital in Iraq.

God knew that soldier and was with him every moment, even at the point of departure from this life.

This isn't just about one lone soldier dying in a foreign land. It is also a story that reminds us of God's presence wherever we are. Whether at home or on a foreign battlefield thousands of miles from people we love, God is always present with us.

One valuable lesson Psalm 139 teaches us is that there is no place in the universe where God isn't present. The psalmist used poetic language to say frequently that God always watches over us. In that watching is divine compassion.

Think of the divine intervention in this simple story. *One* soldier is dying in Baghdad. *One* nurse has a copy of a book that brought her deep solace and she wanted to comfort the boy. God brought the woman with the book and the dying soldier together at exactly the right moment. God intervenes and expresses love in the most unbelievable situations. As the psalmist says, "Every moment you know where I am."

God is present everywhere. As Christians, we say it all the time. But when we have a loved one thousands of miles away and God wraps loving arms around him in his last moments on earth, we're reminded of that reality.

Dear God of life and love, thank you for touching that soldier's life in his final moments. Thank you for that nurse who was present. Thank you for your presence with me today, no matter what I face. Thank you that you'll always reach out to me in my darkest moments. Amen.

The Lord says, "I will rescue those who love me. I will protect those who trust in my name. When they call on me, I will answer; I will be with them in trouble. I will rescue them and honor them."

—Psalm 91:14–15[*]

7

"I NEVER SAW IT COMING"

Life isn't easy and I hear countless tales of suffering and disappointment. Often when people tell me of a disaster they either start or end with a statement like this: "I never saw it coming."

Some of them may not have been willing to see anything negative coming their way; others may have been focused on the wrong things. Regardless, when *it* happens, complete shock takes over and they struggle to cope.

"I never saw the assailant walk into the bank," said one woman who was shot in the face during a robbery and survived.

"I never dreamed my child would drown," said the father of

a two-year-old child who crawled through their fence, waddled into a neighbor's pool, and drowned.

"I never saw the disease coming that would take my wife at age thirty-eight."

All tragic stories, and my heart went out to each person as they related their tales, but none of those stories impacted me as personally as the time I made a phone call to my friend Gary. We had been good friends for years, but I hadn't heard from him for a few weeks. I called and asked, "How are things going?"

"Oh, fine," he said. The tone of his voice signaled something was wrong. Gary didn't say much and I understood the reason: I was his friend and he didn't want to burden me.

"We've known each other for a long time," I said. "I'm your friend. What is going on?"

"My wife left," he said, and his voice cracked. Without warning, his wife had walked out of their home and out of their marriage. She left him with four young children to raise by himself. "I never saw it coming," he said.

I dropped everything at my church and we met that afternoon.

It was a heartbreaking experience and Gary could barely talk about his hurt. The experience was still too raw and overpowering. Right then, he couldn't focus on anything ahead. He was temporarily struck by the immediate blow of his wife's leaving and his sense of loss.

As I listened to my friend, I knew Gary would get beyond

his pain and I knew healing would come, but I also knew Gary hurt right then.

"I never saw it coming," Gary repeated several times.

Gary said it that day. Since then, I've heard it hundreds of times. As I travel around the world, I hear those words from many struggling and confused people. And they tell me how devastated they are. The odd thing is that it doesn't matter whether they saw it coming. If Gary had seen it coming, would the pain have been less? Would the results have been any different? Probably not. Whether tragedy blindsides us or we know before the destruction hurts, the pain is still just as intense.

When I talk about heaven, I often say, "I never saw it coming. How could I have anticipated that a truck would flatten my car and kill me on a bridge?"

While I had no way to see ahead, I do have the responsibility of moving ahead with my own life—of learning how to live with less energy and poorer health than I had before the accident. It's not enough to say, "I never saw it coming." I have to move forward and add, "And now . . ."

We don't have a choice about pain. It's eventually going to come at some time or another. We do, however, have a choice about how to respond. Do we want to stay stuck in a pit of shock, disbelief, pain, and self-pity? Or do we want to tend to our wounds then pick ourselves up and get back on with living?

No, moving on after tragedy is not easy. We need some

help. We need someone stronger to lean on while we slowly get up and start to walk again. We read story after story in the Bible of godly people who endured pain, rejection, heartache, and loss, but they kept on. They could do that because God was with them and they had the assurance of the divine presence. Because of their relationship to a loving Creator, they were able to move beyond not seeing the problem coming and say, "For I can do everything with the help of Christ who gives me the strength I need" (Philippians 4:13*).

Well, guess what? God is with you too. He's with all of us, and with him at your side you can overcome anything.

Wise and loving God, too often I haven't seen the hardships coming, but you have. You don't promise to deflect them; you do promise to comfort me in the midst of my pain and you are with me. For this I thank you. Amen.

[Jesus said,] "That is the way it will be at the end of the world. The angels will come and separate the wicked people from the godly, throwing the wicked into the fire. There will be weeping and gnashing of teeth."

—MATTHEW 13:49–50*

8

"I SMELLED THE SULFUR"

People often share their stories with me. They frequently tell me of their near-death experiences (NDE). In 1992, the Gallup Poll said that approximately eight million Americans claimed to have experienced an NDE. The term *near-death experience* refers to the perception by a person that he or she was clinically dead and revived within a brief period of time.

For the past thirty years, the research has recorded an unusually similar pattern to NDEs. They usually begin with a sense of floating outside and above one's body, then moving upward through a tunnel or narrow space. During an NDE, people often experience a brief but thorough life review ("My whole life flashed before me"). They encounter a bright light and then they see deceased relatives or spiritual figures such as Jesus or Buddha. Immediately they are sent back or pulled back. All of this takes place within a matter of one or two minutes.

I've heard all those stories with few variations. I believe these people had a spiritual experience. They usually tell me that they felt such peace that they were reluctant to return, but a spiritual being told them they had to go back.

Once in a while, however, I hear a different version of an NDE.

Usually they lean down and whisper, "Can I talk to you later? I have something I want to share with you." They have a haunted look, and in a few instances I've seen an expression of outright terror. They want to talk to me but not while anyone else is around. They are the people who went to hell.

The other people, whom I call "the heaven people," usually come and speak quietly and they have a sense of peace about them. But those who experienced hell grapple with whether to talk about it. But because they've finally found somebody—me—who also died, they get the courage to open up.

The first time this happened, a man approached the book-signing table and said, "I had an NDE." I saw terror in his eyes and before I could respond, he added, "And mine wasn't a good experience."

His words shocked me. No one had ever talked to me about a negative NDE.

"You see, I went to hell."

"Tell me about it." I didn't know how else to respond.

"It was awful. I smelled the sulfur and the burning flesh. I felt the heat. I could feel the torment in my body." He went on to say that even though it had happened nearly two years earlier, he had been unable to erase that experience from his mind.

"I'm going to hell," the man said. "God showed me what it would be like, and that's where I'm going."

"You could look at it that way," I said, "or you could see this as God's love at work."

"God's love?" the man sneered.

"Think about it. Instead of a sentence of eternal death, what if God has sent you a warning? What if God wants you to change? What if God wants you to believe and to follow him?"

It was his turn to be surprised.

"When the truck hit me, I went to heaven. I went there because I knew how to get there. Some people go to hell because they don't know how *not* to get there."

I sensed this man wanted me to assure him that he wouldn't spend eternity in such a place. In every instance where I've met such people, every one of them wanted to escape the damnation. They wanted someone to help them realize that heaven was possible for them.

So I encourage them to see that experience as a second

chance at life. They know that they could have stayed in hell and they're grateful that they didn't. In fact, I'm sure they'll be eternally grateful.

Hell is every bit as real as heaven. The response to going there is obviously totally different because these people are glad they lived. They've seen the punishment ahead and it has scared them enough for them to reach toward heaven. I'm glad I'm able to point them in the right direction.

Wise, loving God, you have so many different ways to draw us to yourself. But no matter what method you use, you're always like a caring father, extending your loving arms toward all of us—including me. Sometimes you have to warn or threaten. No matter how you speak to me, please help me hear you and respond to your love. Amen.

The Lord looks down from heaven on the entire human race; he looks to see if there is even one with real understanding, one who seeks for God. But no, all have turned away from God; all have become corrupt. No one does good, not even one!

—PSALM 14:2–3[*]

9

HEAVENLY COMMUNICATION

"What form does communication take in heaven?" That question comes up occasionally. "Do the people speak in English or what language do they use?"

I had to pause and reflect before I could answer. I had no specific memory of the use of English or any other language.

"We did communicate with words, but they weren't English," I said. "I believe it was a heavenly language. Whatever the actual language, it was perfect communication."

That makes sense when you stop to think about it. The big limitation with language is that words are only symbols for our feelings and thoughts. We constantly try to find a better word or we search for a clearer method to say something. When we translate from one language to another, we encounter immense problems. Often we find no exact word in the other language, so we have to speak approximately.

For example, when Cec was a missionary in equatorial Africa, he couldn't talk about snow or freezing temperatures because the people had no concept of being so cold they could die. They don't grow grapes in that part of the world, so he couldn't talk about the fruit of the vine.

It's different in heaven. As I've reflected on my experiences there, I realized no one ever had to say, "I don't understand" or "Explain that again" or "I wonder what he meant by that." Like everything else in heaven, the communication system is flawless. It's perfect.

In heaven, the communication is with words, but it's more than words. All of us understood completely and we knew— we simply knew—the full gravity of one another's emotions and the spiritual depth of what we meant. It was another level of communication. It was a deeper, perfect kind.

We have nothing on earth with which to compare it to. We can't experience heaven on earth because we're not equipped to take in and grasp perfect communication and perfect love.

One way to see this is to go back to the biblical principle

of sin. Before sin came into the world, there must have been perfect communication. If we read the first chapters of Genesis, we find that Adam and God walked together in the Garden of Eden. It may not be clear how that happened, except that it was some form of perfect exchange of ideas between them.

After Adam and Eve sinned, the Bible explains the result by saying their eyes were opened to see their nakedness. From then on, human beings have inherited what we often call *indwelling* sin. It's the imperfection of humanity or the sinfulness in our lives. It's the part of us that darkens our understanding and that makes us selfish and self-centered. This is what Paul means when he writes, "No one is good—not even one . . . All have turned away from God; all have gone wrong" (Romans 3:10–12*). He also says in that oft-quoted verse, "For all have sinned; all fall short of God's glorious standard" (Verse 23).

Heaven is not only the totally ideal place, but a place of miracles. In heaven, our sinfulness is removed. Our eyes are opened; we see, feel, and think perfectly. We become the perfect creation that God intended us to be.

Until then, it's hard to ponder and get any kind of understanding of perfection. Our thoughts center on ourselves, our wants, and our needs. But the day we enter the gates of heaven, all those barriers and hindrances will be removed. We'll be free; we'll be perfect; our communication will be faultless.

God, I can hardly imagine what it will be like to communicate with people from all times and places in heaven. The concept staggers my mind. But then, how can I understand perfection with my imperfect mind? Yet I will, because one day my imperfect mind will become perfect. Thank you. Amen.

I will bless the Lord who guides me; even at night my heart instructs me. I know the Lord is always with me. I will not be shaken, for he is right beside me.

—Psalm 16:7–8*

10

MISSING THEM

"You've helped me realize how joyful and contented people are in heaven and that it's okay not to miss them." That's typical of e-mails I receive. People are worried about their loved ones, wanting reassurance that those who have gone on ahead aren't sorrowing or suffering.

One of my friends said, "That's laughable. How could they not know their loved ones are happy?"

On the surface, it may sound laughable, but I try to ask, what's the question behind the question? Why is that person worried about a loved one who has already gone to heaven?

Obviously, there are many reasons, but one of them seems patently obvious: They miss that person. One woman said, "My husband and I were married for forty-two years." She told me he had died two years earlier, "but I still miss him. Every day I think about him."

That's natural. Then she leaned close and whispered, "Do you think he's really all right?"

"He's perfect" was my answer.

She could think only from her perspective, that of being without her mate and missing him. She wasn't able to focus on him and his blissful state.

"Maybe so," she said and her eyes moistened. "I still miss him. I wish, oh, I wish I could talk to him or get a message to him—"

"What would you say to him if you could?" I asked. Her startled look made me realize she hadn't considered the content. "What would you say? Would it be, 'I miss you and I'm lonely? I'm sorry you died. I don't do as well as I used to because you're not here with me?' Is that the message you want to send?"

"Oh, no!"

"Think of it this way," I said as kindly as I knew how. "There's no communication we have here that they need to understand. Any message we send could only bring sadness to them. It would make them miss us or worry about us. If they missed us or worried about us, it wouldn't be heaven, would it?"

"I know," she said sadly, "but still . . . I wish I could let him know how much I miss him."

I understood what she meant. She was still focused on her

grief and her sense of loss. We didn't have time to talk at length, but I prayed for her and asked God to help her focus on *his* peace and *his* utter joy. I closed the prayer with these words: "And may she remember that he'll be at the gate to welcome her when she arrives."

Heavenly Father, thank you that my loved ones who have entered heaven before me are happy and joyfully contented. Because I miss them, remind me that you are perfect and our heavenly home is perfect because you're there. They have no pain, no worries, and no heartaches. Fill me with peace and hopeful assurance as I look heavenward for my own journey. Amen.

Whatever happens, dear brothers and sisters, may the
Lord give you joy. I never get tired of telling you this.
I am doing this for your own good.

—PHILIPPIANS 3:1*

11
I DIDN'T WANT TO RETURN

"I didn't want to come back to Earth," I said several times.

Those words shocked my father-in-law. "What about Eva and the children? Didn't you want to see them?"

"No," I said. "Heaven isn't like that."

I explained to him as I try to say to others that in heaven we don't miss anyone. Of course, I was only there a short time, but I'm convinced my attitude would have been the same if I had stayed longer. While we're alive on Earth, we think of things we'll miss and people from whom we'll be separated.

For example, often people are physically ready to die but they keep holding on because they think the family needs them, or that someone depends on them. Sometimes family members have to give them permission to surrender to death.

But once death comes and they enter into heaven, all their values change. "Why would anyone want to return?" I sometimes respond when people ask me about my desire to stay in heaven.

"We can't miss anyone," I often say, "because we have no awareness that they're not there." That statement may not make a lot of sense to some people, but it's true. The quality of life is perfect—it's like a celebration that never ends. People don't sit around and worry about what might have been or take attendance to figure out who didn't show up for the event.

"When you want to be *there*," I've said many times, "you never want to be alive *here*."

We miss them because we're still here, but they don't miss us and that's not a bad thing. It's true that if I had thought about my family back on earth, I would have felt despondent. I would have missed them and worried about them and probably fretted over the decisions they made, and above all else, I would have wanted only good things for them. But I didn't think about them, not once.

Had I thought of them, it would have been a situation like the Israelites after they left Egypt. God provided for them and for all of their needs, including food. Their clothes never wore out, and God protected them from the weather as they traveled. What God didn't do was erase their memories. Despite God's abundant food supply, they moaned about what they didn't have to eat. One time they complained, "We remember the fish we ate in Egypt at no cost—also the cucumbers, melons, leeks, onions, and garlic" (Numbers 11:5**).

God provided, but they remembered. As long as their minds returned to the past, the more miserable and unhappy they became. In fact, I imagine that the Israelites missed their cucumbers and garlic so much that eventually they began to idealize life in Egypt. They forgot they had been slaves—they had banished thoughts of beatings and denied their cries to God to set them free. They could remember only the good things back in Egypt—or what they remembered as good.

Heaven is different. Heaven erases the memory of garlic, leeks, onions, and everything else. Heaven is perfect because everything there is flawless and we need nothing.

We can never enjoy heaven on earth, but we can move a little closer if we choose. The apostle Paul certainly presents a living example to us. He wrote to the church at Philippi while imprisoned by the Romans. He had no idea whether he would live or die. Instead of fretting over *his* situation, he expressed concern over *theirs*. That's why he writes about being content no matter where he was. He also writes, "Yes, everything is worthless when compared with the priceless gain of knowing Christ Jesus my Lord. I have discarded everything else, counting it all as garbage, so that I may have Christ and become one with him" (Philippians 3:8–9a*).

We may not reach the level of contentment and inner peace that Paul did, but he certainly points the way. The more we turn our eyes heavenward, the more we prepare ourselves for the perfect life ahead.

God, I find it easy to think about what I don't have or what I've lost—in fact, it's easier to dwell on those things than it is to concentrate on what I have now. Help me. Enable me to focus on what lies ahead and not to look back. Amen.

[Job asked,] ". . . Should we accept only good things from the hand of God and never anything bad?"
So in all this, Job said nothing wrong.

—JOB 2:10[*]

12

GETTING KNOCKED DOWN

A large number of letters and e-mails come from people who feel despondent. "I'm so depressed, I don't know if I'll ever get over it" is a phrase that appears in many of the letters. "I'm ready to hang it up," read one e-mail.

A woman e-mailed, "I lost my mother and my husband left me." That was only the first sentence. From there she listed about a dozen heartaches and disappointments. "I've missed so much work because of all my problems that every week I expect to get fired." She ended her litany with these words, "If it wasn't for my three kids, I'd take my own life. I won't do that because I don't know what would happen to them."

That's sad, and it's such a tragedy. She may also have some serious psychological problems, but that's not the point I want to make. I prefer to focus on the fact that the woman hurt—and she hurt enough to reach out to a virtual stranger. Her pain was so intense and she had become so desperate that she had contemplated suicide.

Sometimes I wish I could stare into the eyes of all those despondent souls in the world and say, "Okay, life has knocked you down. You don't have to stay down. You can get up and keep fighting."

In her own way, that woman continues to fight. Because she has three children, she's able to hold on. She has a reason to continue. Perhaps knowing her children need her and that she's responsible for them may be enough for her to gradually get back on her feet.

I never want to judge other people, and I have no idea what goes on inside their heads and hearts. One thing, however, occurs to me. So many of us grumble and complain when things run amok. I don't think that's totally wrong. After all, who wants to shout and rejoice over misery? But I do think we need to be consistent. If we're going to whine about the bad things, then consistency says we need to pause and give thanks for the good things such as when we have a good day. Be thankful for days when we're free of pain or feel healthy. What about when we feel loved? Isn't it wonderful when someone makes us feel important? Isn't it marvelous to reach the end of a day and feel we've accomplished important things and we're now relaxed? Do we give thanks for our families? Do we rejoice that we have jobs? This list could become almost endless. Some of us may have to seek harder, but we can always find causes for giving thanks.

I love the attitude of Job. He lost just about everything in his life, but he held on with an upbeat attitude. His attitude was that if we're going to grab hold of the good in life, we also need to accept the bad.

Perhaps it's because we don't grasp the good and appreciate what we do have that we fall so emotionally low when the bad hits.

All-wise God, at times I don't know your will, even though I'd like to know. Most of all, I need to know that you will give me the strength to get up every time life knocks me down. With your strength I can keep on fighting and for this I thank you. Amen.

[Jesus said,] *"In my Father's house are many rooms;*
if it were not so, I would have told you. I am going
there to prepare a place for you."

—JOHN 14:2**

13

IT'S REAL

Heaven is real. Most Christians believe that—or at least they want to believe. People throw questions at me about heaven. One of the most commonly asked is simply: "Is heaven real?"

When they ask, I think they already believe in the place of eternal bliss, but they want assurance and they want to know what it's like being there.

"It's the most real place I know" is my standard answer. I usually add, "Since my visit there, it's the standard by which I judge everything that I feel, smell, touch, see, and hear here." I also tell them that sometimes life on earth doesn't seem real anymore. Everything feels so temporal—and it is. What is today passes away and what happens tomorrow also passes.

For me, the experience was so powerful and so lasting I have no trouble talking about what heaven is like. Although I had always believed in heaven because I believed in Jesus Christ and the words of the Bible, now that I have been there, any doubts or questions have been erased.

I also understand people's questions. They want assurance. They want to know that the injustices, inequities, and hardships of this life aren't the final acts. They want to know that every failure and shortcoming in their own lives will be wiped away.

The first disciples had similar questions. They had traveled with Jesus for three years, witnessed miracles (and performed a few themselves), and heard his marvelous teachings.

Even so, their doubts didn't fully disappear. Even after the resurrection, when Jesus appeared to his disciples, they had doubts. Matthew writes, "Then the eleven disciples went to Galilee, to the mountain where Jesus had told them to go. When they saw him, they worshiped him; but some doubted" (Matthew 28:16–17**). *But some doubted*. Even then. Even after they had seen him crucified and now resurrected, they still harbored questions. Maybe that's just part of being human.

Jesus understood their doubts. When he talked to them about the rooms in his Father's house, he began by saying, "Do not let your hearts be troubled. Trust in God; trust also in me" (John 14:1**).

They wanted to believe—but despite everything they experienced as Jesus' disciples, doubts persisted. Maybe that's the way human nature is. Even if we believe with all our hearts, doubts still trouble and nibble away at the corners of our minds.

Perhaps that's also the reason many ask, "Is heaven real?" They know the answer; they want me to say the words. Among the people who ask are those whose loved ones have died, or whose marriages have fallen apart, or those who have suffered some other loss. They want hope. They want assurance that this life isn't the end.

The most difficult times for people to believe and the time they need the most comfort is when life turns upside down, when adversity knocks them over the head and they're confused and uncertain about their day-to-day living.

One man, with tears in his eyes, asked about the reality of heaven. He was fifty-four years old, his company had recently merged with a large corporation, and he had been told, "In three weeks, your job no longer exists."

"Yes, heaven is real," I told him, "but you have to make a reservation." I made my reservation at age sixteen. The youth minister from my church came to my home and showed me how to make my eternal reservation. At age thirty-eight, when the big truck hit me, I went to the place that I had prepared for: heaven. That was no surprise to me.

Heaven is real; it truly is the most real place I know. If you haven't already done so, make your reservation now. You will be assured a room in heaven.

God of eternal love, I believe your promises. I trust you and know that you sent Jesus Christ to die for my sins. I want to confirm my reservation and I look forward to the greeting committee at the gate to usher me into my room. Thank you for your assurance. Amen.

Every human being has an earthly body just like Adam's, but our heavenly bodies will be just like Christ's. Just as we are now like Adam, the man of the earth, so we will someday be like Christ, the man from heaven.

—1 Corinthians 15:48–49*

14

"Give Me a Sign"

Maybe it's human nature to want signs; maybe we seek concrete evidence to bolster our faith. Whatever the reason, I often hear people say, "Oh, if God would only give me a sign, then all my doubts would go away."

It's probably not true that all doubts would vanish, but I understand the yearning for a sign. I find this is especially true with some people when they mourn the death of a loved one. Maybe they want a sign that the person went to be with Jesus Christ and not to the place of torment. Maybe they seek assurance to boost their own faith.

Although God occasionally gives signs, that's not the way the Christian faith works. If we believe, we have the inner certainty that God is trustworthy and eventually will make all things right.

Sometimes people want a sign from heaven so badly, they'll grab on to anything that feels, looks, or acts like a divine message. For instance, a man said, "I felt as if God sent my son to visit me recently."

He said he had been in deep grief over the loss of his son. He prayed for God to speak to him and to assure him that his son was all right. "That afternoon, I stood in front of my house, and I saw a monarch butterfly. It fluttered around me two or three times, maybe ten feet away, but as I stared at it, I thought, 'That's my son who has come back to show me that he's all right. He's in a better place and wants to comfort me. He wants me to know he's free and happy.'"

Although it wasn't easy for me to tell him, I said, "No, that wasn't your son in the form of a butterfly."

Tears filled his eyes as if I were trying to steal his inner peace.

"That butterfly might be a way for you to find peace. You saw the butterfly and as you watched it fly around, you thought about your son. Those thoughts eased your pain, right?"

He nodded.

"As you watched it glide around gracefully, it brought you the peaceful assurance that he is in God's hands. Wasn't that enough? Why do you need to read something into that? If that butterfly can calm your heart and diminish your grief, isn't it enough to thank God and to see it was a means toward your healing?"

Another time a woman told me that her daughter died and the next day a cardinal appeared at her bird feeder and returned every day for more than a month. "Could that be the spirit of my daughter, who returned in such a magnificent form? Or was it a special sign of comfort to me from God? By the time the bird stopped coming, I was able to move past the worst part of my pain." She also pointed out that red was her daughter's favorite color.

I don't want to make light of the woman's grief or diminish the impact of the comfort she received, but I have to say that was definitely not her daughter's spirit and it wasn't a special sign from her daughter. However, God can and does use many means to comfort us.

When we see a butterfly or a bird or any other creation of God, those things might help us in our sorrow and to cope with our loss. There are no such supernatural signs mentioned in the Bible. The daughter didn't fly back as a bird or anything else. There is no reincarnation (or more technically, the transmigration of souls). God created each of as a human being with one soul. We will always be human beings and nothing else. God will give us glorified bodies, according to Paul's words in 1 Corinthians 15, but we'll always remain human.

I don't mean this as a negative and judgmental statement. I don't want to take away anyone's comfort, but I don't want to give people false comfort either. Instead, I want people to think of the kindness and love of God. I want them to ponder how wonderfully God uses various means—even monarch butterflies or cardinals—to brighten the lives of the sad, grieving parents and hasten their inner healing. I have no trouble accepting the fact that God helped them focus on something that reminded them of his loving presence and goodness as a means to help them through their pain.

God doesn't send people back in other forms; God does send encouragement. God does reach out to us and speak to us through nature, through music, through literature, or any other means he chooses. And the purpose is to heal our pain.

God, at times, I'd like to have signs to encourage and strengthen me. But I also know that my loved ones are not just in good hands—they're in perfect hands. I can trust them into your keeping. They're fully happy and fully alive because they're with you. Thank you for encouraging me. Amen.

And remember that the heavenly Father to whom you pray has no favorites when he judges. He will judge or reward you according to what you do. So you must live in reverent fear of him during your time as foreigners here on earth.

—1 Peter 1:17*

15
GOD'S FAVORITES

He wore a T-shirt that read: *God loves you but I'm his favorite.* It was a joke, of course. All of us know that God has no favorites. At least we say we believe that.

Emotionally, however, we may not be sure. "Why does he have such an easy life and I have to slave so hard?" I've heard words of envy and jealousy because others have what we want. "I'm as bright (or as deserving or as hard a worker) as she is. But she has the job and I don't."

Despite all the statements in the Bible and all the common sense that goes with knowing we serve a just and honorable God, at some point, most of us pause and at least wonder why we have hardships.

Perhaps an illustration helps. Years ago, a friend named Verna complained about the inequities of her life. "I just think God has his picks. He just plain likes some people better." No matter how I or anyone else reasoned with Verna, she was convinced that she wasn't one of God's favorites.

What kind of life would Verna (or anyone else) have had if she had truly been God's favorite? We think of those great figures mentioned in the Bible such as David in the Old Testament and the apostle Paul in the New Testament. If God truly favored them, what kind of lives would they have had?

We know the answer. We only have to ask, "How did God treat David?"

God gave the young man the ability to kill a lion with his bare hands and he later killed Goliath with his sling. After that, the prophet-priest Samuel anointed him king over Israel. But if we follow the story, it's not a smooth ride. King Saul tried to impale him with a spear. David ran away, and for years Saul tried to kill him. David was at least a middle-aged man before he became king. Is that an example of God's favoritism?

Perhaps it truly is. Perhaps if there is anything such as being special to God (and some might interpret it as being a favorite), along with that favor or grace we find hardship, trials, and problems.

Paul seems the best New Testament candidate for being a favorite of God. In 2 Corinthians 11, he tells about all his many near-encounters with death and the years of persecution and beatings. That's some kind of favoritism.

Is it possible that the hardships and sufferings in our lives not only have purpose (and I believe they do), but they also draw us closer to God? Is it possible that the heavier our burdens, the closer God's spirit hovers? Is it possible that the more hardships we face, the more opportunities we have to feel like God's favorites?

I think so.

God, I know you don't have favorites, but sometimes I've wondered why I have so many problems. Help me to think of the hardships that come my way as opportunities to grow. But also, help me to see that they show your closeness because you're there to deliver and encourage me and to hold my hand as I go through them. Amen.

*The wolf will live with the lamb, the leopard will lie down
with the goat, the calf and the lion and the yearling
together . . . They will neither harm nor destroy on all my
holy mountain, for the earth will be full of the knowledge
of the Lord as the waters cover the sea.*

—Isaiah 11:6, 9**

16

ANIMALS IN HEAVEN?

One question I often get is this: "Are there animals in heaven?" "When you were being greeted by all your loved ones and people who were significant in your life on Earth, were there any animals present?"

People are confused because some say there are no animals in heaven because they don't have souls. Others say there are animals in heaven because they are mentioned in the Bible.

Here's what I say: First, I didn't see any animals, but that doesn't preclude their being there. People met me—people who had been instrumental in my coming to faith and growing in faith. No animals had been significant in my spiritual life.

Second, the Bible speaks about animals in the renewed Earth, which some call a millennium on Earth. A long section of Isaiah 11 refers to predators like lions, bears, snakes, and leopards living peacefully alongside the domesticated cows, oxen, lambs, and even a child.

The animals may be purely symbolic and poetic, because the Bible offers no definitive statement; however, I believe there will be animals in heaven, even though I didn't see them myself.

Third, and this is what's important: Heaven is a place of perfection. Whatever our needs, God will provide for them. If it takes animals to enhance our joy, we can be sure that God will provide. It's not so much what or who is or isn't in heaven. What is important is that we will be there for eternity. We'll relish every moment and we won't miss what's on earth. If it happens that there are no animals in heaven, we won't miss our pets.

I understand why this question comes up often. People love their pets. For some, they have become like members of the family. Those animals bring peace and comfort. "I can't imagine heaven without my dog," one woman said. If that's what she needs, God will provide pets.

Although, I honestly don't know for sure because I didn't see any animals in heaven, I believe they will be present. My reason is because I see their importance in human history. One of the first tasks Adam and Eve had before them was to name the animals: "So the Lord God formed from the soil every kind of animal and bird. He brought them to Adam to see what he would call them, and Adam chose a name for each one. He gave names to all the livestock, birds, and wild animals" (Genesis 2:19–20*). I also believe that animals are part of God's creation and all creation will be present in perfect form.

Other questions come up that are just as powerful to some people. They want to know what trees or plants I saw. My answer is simple: I was so caught up with the people, the music, and the joy of heaven, I didn't pay attention to anything else.

The main focus in heaven is the presence of God. In heaven, we'll all know each other and we'll be able to speak the same language. It has to be that way to be a place of perfection.

We also know that God is the perfect host. Jesus Christ will be there. God will lavishly provide for every need we have. Nothing will be missing. After all, if anything is missing, it won't be heaven, will it?

God of heaven and earth, I find it easy to focus on questions about heaven and what it will be like. Help me focus on being fully ready for the final journey and to be prepared to enter into the "joy unspeakable and full of glory" (1 Peter 1:8†).

And if we have hope in Christ only for this life,
we are the most miserable people in the world.

—1 Corinthians 15:19*

17

But Not My Spirit

"A woman e-mailed me about her experience with cancer. She had surgery to remove large tumors, followed by six months of treatment. Yet she wrote, "I lost my hair and my energy, but not my spirit."

As I read those words, her last phrase struck me—*"but not my spirit."* This woman, like many others, testifies to the strength and the character of people who face tremendous odds.

Why do some people stand up against the strongest odds and keep on going when others around them have given up or fallen? Some fall under the slightest pressure, while others say, "As long as I breathe, don't count me down and permanently out."

Over the years I've heard or read many stories of powerful internal stamina by people who stood against the odds. As I mentioned earlier, after World War II, Viktor Frankl wrote of his experiences in a Nazi concentration camp. He noticed that the hope factor enabled men to remain alive. As long as they believed they had something to live for, such as being united with a loved one—regardless of the opposition, the starvation, the physical toll—they survived.

He also pointed out that when a man would receive word that his wife or child had died—the focus of his hope—within a few days that person just gave up and also died.

Frankl emphasized the significance of hope—of something ahead to anticipate, of looking forward. Such hope enabled those men to endure their ongoing trauma. As Paul said, "And if we have hope in Christ only for this life, we are the most miserable people in the world." He could write that because he was a man who had endured persecution and many times fled for his life, but always he trusted in something yet ahead—the joy of living forever with Jesus Christ.

Even if we don't go through what Paul or Viktor Frankl went through, even if we don't have cancer and don't have to suffer through surgery and treatment, we have our own particular difficulties and hardships. I believe God gives us only as heavy a load as we're able to handle. The result, of course, is that afterward we're stronger. We're the ones who can encourage and strengthen others in their hardships.

I realize now that I shouldn't question God about why certain things happen—especially to good people. I know that good and bad come into every life. What we need to remember is that God will give us the strength to get through any ordeal.

Dear God, I don't like the problems I face, and at times I wish I didn't have to go through the troubles ahead of me. Remind me that your strength is mine, that your grace is enough, and that I will survive every challenge. Amen.

Many sorrows come to the wicked, but unfailing love surrounds those who trust the Lord.

—Psalm 32:10*

18

Symptoms

I often think of a story I heard from a professor at the New Orleans Baptist Theological Seminary. His office door burst open and a student raced in with the secretary behind him. The man pounded the professor's desk and yelled because of the unjust way he was being treated. The secretary apologized. "I'm so sorry. I did everything I could to keep him out. Should I call security?"

"No, it's all right," the professor said calmly. He told the young man to sit down and tell him what had upset him. After ten minutes of listening, the professor said, "I'd like you to come back tomorrow at two o'clock. Please come right on into my office. By then I'll have additional information and I'll be prepared to discuss anything you have to say."

"You'd better be," the man said and stood up. "I've got

some things—big things I want to say!" He turned, stalked out of the room, and banged the door.

When the professor told his secretary that the student would return the next day, she was quite upset. "His behavior was terrible." She suggested he have security guards at the door.

He waved aside the idea. "That was only a symptom; that wasn't the problem. He hurts and he has something he wants to talk to me about, and we'll discuss it tomorrow. He needs someone to listen to his pain, so I look forward to talking to him."

That simple story taught me something. The professor didn't condemn or judge. He was able to see beyond the rage, and most of all, he recognized that the anger directed at him wasn't really the problem.

The young man needed hope. He needed someone to care and to listen. When he returned the next day, the student was calm and apologized for his actions the previous day. Before he left, he shook the professor's hand.

We all respond differently to setbacks in life. Some sink inward into depression. Others become enraged. Occasionally a few become stoic. Regardless of the emotional reactions, they are symptoms of bigger problems.

What I've also learned is that we can't choose the problems that beset us, but we can choose our responses. We learned early to make choices when we were disappointed, rejected, or hurt. We tend to think they're normal, natural, and irreversible. That's not true. We can learn to change the way we react to tragedy and heartache. We can learn new approaches to old problems. That's one reason I often recommend counseling of some kind—talking to someone who is not emotionally tied up in the problem. We can let that person speak objectively and guide us to handle our situation differently than we did in the past. We may need a support group or a change of associates, anything that will enable us to seriously rethink how we want to respond to life's heartaches.

For instance, it's not uncommon for someone to say, "I've lost my sister. She was the best friend I've ever had in my life. I don't know how I'll live without her." Some individuals are so wrapped up in their grief, they're convinced they can never be happy again.

"But there'll never be another person like her," one grieving woman said.

"No, there won't be," I agreed. "Don't try to substitute someone else, but those same emotions and skills that bound you in a relationship with her are what you can use to establish new relationships."

Too often people remain so focused on how they feel that they don't realize they can move beyond their pain. "Think of it this way," I told one grieving father, "God enabled you to feel the pain of loss. You hurt. As you felt those symptoms, you faced your deep loss. If you'll allow it to happen, the pain will lessen. You won't ever forget your daughter, but you can move beyond the symptom of grief."

God, yes, I've confused symptoms with the problems. Help me realize that the pain, the anger, the distress I feel may be your way to help me focus on my hurt and that you will help me move beyond that. Thank you for help and for hope. Amen.

Give discernment to me, your servant;
then I will understand your decrees.

—PSALM 119:125*

19

BEING DIFFERENT

Sometimes people stare at me, and I don't like it—even if I do understand. After my heavenly trip and despite my thirty-four surgeries, I still have physical problems. There are a number of things I can't do and certain body postures I can't emulate.

One of the first times I became aware of being different was when my twin sons and I went to a shoe repair store in a Houston mall. Since the accident I've had to wear an inch-high lift on my left shoe.

I stood at the counter and a man was there with his son. My sons were in their early teens and I assumed that boy was about the same age. The clerk turned to me and asked, "Can I help you?"

"I need to have a heel lift put on this left shoe, about an inch."

"You don't want them on both shoes?"

"No, I just want it on the left shoe."

"You sure you don't want it on both shoes?" he repeated.

The other customer and his son stared at me.

"No, just the left shoe. My left leg is about an inch and a half shorter than my right leg."

"Oh," he said and took the shoe.

The man and his son immediately stared at my legs. They weren't courteous enough to look away.

"Why are you staring at our dad?" my son Chris asked the boy.

The kid didn't answer, but he kept staring.

When the clerk returned with my shoe, I paid and pulled my sons out of the store. I admitted they were right that the man and his son had been insensitive. The cobbler had been just as insensitive. It shouldn't have mattered to him why I wanted only one lift.

Chris said the boy stared at us as we walked down the mall.

"I can't believe he did that," Joe said.

"Well, boys, being different always attracts attention. It just does," I said. "It doesn't mean anything, they're just curious."

"It was uncalled for," Chris insisted. "I just can't believe it."

"Maybe you're just a little more sensitive than most people, but you have to accept the fact that sometimes things happen to you when you do become different, you look different, you are different."

As I thought more about it, I said, "Our society is so homogenized and focused on uniformity that when somebody is different it does attract attention. So you're just going to have to accept that."

That experience happened years ago, but, obviously, I've never forgotten. When I see people who are different, that memory races back. Sometimes those people have obvious physical disfigurements. They're on crutches or they walk with a cane or maybe they're in a wheelchair the way I was once. Whatever it is, they are outwardly different.

People need to understand that sometimes the things that happen will make them permanently different, either on the inside or the outside. Every one of us is changed by our experiences. I know people who had bad teeth for years and were self-conscious about their smiles. They either had their teeth fixed or got dentures, but they still maintained that self-conscious smile. A woman, badly injured in an accident as a teen, had an ugly scar across her cheek. Years later she had the scar removed, but she couldn't remove the invisible scar and constantly covered that part of her face with her hand.

That's often how life works. Some are different in the more obvious ways. All of us are different in some ways. We need to learn to accept those differences, otherwise they become significant issues that bind us or hinder us throughout life. The dyslexic tries to conform, can't, and becomes frustrated. Once she learns there are tricks to help, her reading and writing improve. My friend with Tourette's can't stop the tics and body jerks, but he's learned to accept that's who he is.

That's the healthiest way: Accept who we are. I don't celebrate my injuries, but I try to accept them. If people are curious and ask questions, I'm glad to answer. Instead of emphasizing how badly I was injured, I celebrate what a great job doctors did putting me back together again.

I decided to be upbeat. I sometimes have to say, "No, my elbow won't straighten out, and no, my hand won't turn over, but I still have my arm and I can shake hands." I smile and say, "I can still put my arm around someone." I try to think of the things I can do, and not focus on what I can't do.

In those moments, I also realize that it really is all right to be different—God loves me and accepts me just as I am, and I don't have to change anything for him.

God, I'm alive. I can function and I can also choose how I face my situation. I can focus on being different, inferior, or not conforming. Or I can focus on the good things in life that I can celebrate. Help me to realize that no matter how different I may appear to others, I am still loved by you. Thank you. Amen.

*[Joshua said,] "But if you are unwilling to serve the Lord,
then choose today whom you will serve . . . -
But as for me and my family, we will serve the Lord."*
—JOSHUA 24:15[*]

20

THE RESULTS OF DECISIONS

The Bible presents a powerful, dramatic scene of the end of Joshua's life. The aging leader faced the people and challenged them to make a decision. He told them either to serve God or to serve the pagan influences around him, but that he and his family were committed to God.

Most of us don't have those big decisions often. For most of us, it's like the dancer and choreographer Agnes de Mille said, "No trumpets sound when the important decisions of our life are made. Destiny is made known silently."

We make choices every day and most of them seem insignificant and perhaps trivial. Most of the time we have no way to foresee that those simple choices will alter our lives. For instance, when I drove away from the Trinity Pines Conference

Center, I had a choice of which way to drive to reach Alvin, the Houston bedroom community where I lived and where I was the pastor. I could have chosen Highway 59 and headed west. That was the way I had always gone. The other way was to take the Gulf Freeway—I-45 to Houston. The distance was about the same.

I made a choice with no concerted effort and didn't pray for guidance or hear a voice say, "Go that way." It seemed like a simple decision. But after I made the choice, there was no way I could have known that an eighteen-wheeler would crash into my Ford at 11:45 that morning while I was on the middle of the bridge. Hundreds of times over the years, I've thought of how life would have been different if I had decided to take the other route.

I had made a decision. An accident was the result. Aside from the big choices such as a career change or getting married, rarely do we realize the seriousness of our choices. Only when things go wrong do we look back and ask, "What if I had . . . ?" "But if I had only . . . ?" We can't undo those events, and we need to be mindful that every decision has consequences—even decisions as simple as choosing which seat to take on a bus or which flight to book to reach a destination.

Who would have dreamed of the results that would follow my simple option to take one road instead of the other?

But think of this: Who would have believed that I could tell my story and that lives would be eternally different? That people would make life-changing decisions based on listening to me share my experiences?

Next to my death-to-life experience, the one decision that most changed my life happened when I was sixteen years old. I accepted an invitation from three people I didn't know. After that, I could never go back to my former way of life.

I lived in Bossier, Louisiana, a city across the river from Shreveport. One summer afternoon, the doorbell rang. My mother went to the front door and I heard her ask, "Who?" Then she turned around and called, "Don, there are three kids here to see you."

I went to the door and there stood a boy and two girls. They introduced themselves as Barry, Carmen, and Jan. Because of those three teens, I began to attend church and eventually made a decision to become a Christian. But my salvation story started with the simple act of talking to three high school students. The decision at sixteen determined where I went when I died in the car accident. There is another place people go when they die, and that could have been my destiny.

In the hundreds of times I've thought about my life, I can always see the loving hand of God stretched out toward me. God sought me and I surrendered when I had no serious problems. When the really big moment in my life came, I was ready because I had chosen correctly.

God, I have no idea why some things happen or how minor decisions determine my destiny. But I do know you're involved in my life, even in those dark moments. Remind me of your love, which never leaves me. Amen.

Forgetting what is behind and straining toward what is ahead, I press on toward the goal to win the prize for which God has called me heavenward in Christ Jesus.

—PHILIPPIANS 3:13–14**

21

THE WAY IT USED TO BE

"I'm praying for your *total* healing," the e-mail began.

I receive such e-mails regularly—and I appreciate them. People are mightily concerned about my health and sometimes they should be because everything in my body doesn't work well. I rarely think about what I can't do. That's not denial—I decided not to focus on what I can't do and emphasize what I can.

I appreciate their compassion and their concern. And I'd be a total fool not to want a healed body. Can my healing actually happen on Earth? Absolutely, because God has never gone out of the miracle business. Will it happen on this earth? Probably not.

I don't want to limit God in any way; and if physical healing is in my future, I'll make my reservation now. What I don't want to do is to get so caught up in asking for healing that it diverts my energy and my attention from the ministry God has given me.

It's frustrating at times not to be able to do the things I once did. I don't get really angry, but such things catch up with me. I'll start to do something that is routine for most people and I realize I can't. It's like a thorn in the flesh or a reminder. Even though I want to do something and intend to, it won't happen. I don't think that's very different from many people who face physical limitations because of birth defects, accidents, disease, or aging. If we don't come to grips with our limits, we can become depressed—and many people do sink into deep depression.

I'm fairly aware of what I can't do and I don't like it, but that's the way it is. Most people learn to avoid what they can't do. That's common sense.

But what we don't want to do is spend our time bemoaning our current condition, yearning for life the way it used to be, and trying to manipulate everything we can to get back to that state again. The old way is not going to return and we know that—even if we still secretly long for the way it used to be.

Hope—or expectation—is a positive approach to what is now and what the future holds. It's a way to say, "Yes, life isn't perfect and it isn't everything I want it to be, but one day it will be perfect. One day—the day I ascend to heaven—all will be flawless and better than I could have imagined."

I'd like people to continue to pray for my healing, but I want to be free to take the message of hope to others. Despite my weakened body and my physical limits, I can still say, "God is with me. The best is yet to be."

I want to be like the apostle Paul. He had all the privileges of a high-born Jew, but instead of capitalizing on that he said he forgot those things and pushed them behind him. That's the only way he could push ahead. We can't drive forward if our eyes stay focused on the rearview mirror.

God, erase from my heart the way things used to be, especially when I concentrate on them and become miserable and want things to be the way they once were. Instead, help me keep my eyes focused upward—focused on you and the perfection that lies ahead. Amen.

. . . And God is faithful . . .

—I CORINTHIANS 10:13*

22

COMPARED TO YOU

The woman sat in the front row of the church when I spoke, and afterward she stood in line to get an autograph. After she bought three copies of *90 Minutes in Heaven* to give away, she told me a little about herself. She was a single parent and raised two severely mentally disabled sons. That Sunday evening was the first time in a month she had been able to leave them with anyone.

Abruptly she stopped telling me about her problems and said, "Oh, Mr. Piper, I'm sorry for rambling like this. Compared to what happened to you, my experience is nothing."

Her words shocked me, even though I understood what she was trying to say. "Really?" I asked. "Compared to you, I think my life is probably much easier."

I don't want to compare what happened to me with the woes of anyone else. That's not how God works or how he wants us to think about life. I don't want to compare my life, my struggles, or my hardships with anyone else's. I want people to know that mountains and valleys appear in each of our lives. The geography is different, but the landscape is largely the same. We all have hardships—that's just part of being human.

We should take the life God showers on us and thank him for what we can, pray for help for what we can't handle, and praise the Lord that we survive and thrive each day. Some people carry heavy burdens—burdens I'm sure I couldn't handle. But then, everyone couldn't have gone through what I did. That's where the difference comes in and it's a good reason to avoid comparison. Because we're different by temperament and ability, we're also different in the amount of adversity we can handle.

Perhaps a better way to think about our heavy loads is to pause and give thanks to God that we're able to cope with the demands of today. We don't know how well we'll do tomorrow or the week after that, but we know we can make it through today.

What if we saw our individual burdens as exactly the right load that God feels we can handle? What if we pondered this thought? *This is exactly the life God wants me to have.*

"And God is faithful," the apostle wrote. Although the context is about handling temptations, the principle applies to hardships or problems as well: "But remember that the temptations that come into your life are no different from what others experience. And God is faithful. He will keep the temptation from becoming so strong that you can't stand up against it. When you are tempted, he will show you a way out so that you will not give in to it" (1 Corinthians 10:13*).

God is faithful. That means faithful in rushing to my help, but it also means faithful in giving me only the amount of pain I can bear—never too much for me to handle with his help.

Yes, God is faithful.

Incomparable God, forgive me for comparing my situation with others. Whatever load you give me, remind me that it is exactly what I need right now and you're with me to see that I can carry whatever load you give me. Amen.

Be joyful always; pray continually; give thanks in all
circumstances, for this is God's will for you in Jesus Christ.
—1 THESSALONIANS 5:16–18**

23
AM I GLAD I DIED?

"Aren't you glad you died, went to heaven, and came back again?" she asked with a wide grin. At first I thought she was joking, until she added, "I wish it had happened to me."

"No, you don't wish it had happened to you." I tried (probably unsuccessfully) to point out the pain I endured. I told her that the first days after I returned, no one knew whether I would live. During those 108 days in the hospital, I went through more pain than I felt any human ought to suffer. "I'd like to be the old Don Piper again and function like a normal human being," I said. "No, I'm not glad."

And yet there is an element of truth when she asked, "Aren't you glad?" I doubt that I can ever say, "Thanks, God, for letting a truck hit me." I do, however, rejoice at what I've been able to do *because* that truck hit me.

Probably no one is more amazed than I am at what God has done with my life and my message since the accident. For nearly fifteen years I didn't say anything to anyone, but once I began to speak, people listened. Cec helped me write my story and a publisher bought it. Since then, I've had speaking opportunities all over the world. God has used my testimony and I can't help but rejoice in all the wonderful things that have happened. That's not the same as being thankful for the accident.

This also doesn't mean that my life would have been second class if it hadn't happened. I was a pastor and I was on my way to church to preach that evening. I was already serving Jesus Christ the best I knew how. I have no idea what my life would be like today if it had not been for the accident, and it's not anything I want to waste energy considering. Instead, I think of the privilege God has given me to travel widely and bring the message of hope to others.

I had to go through that ordeal to be where I am today. I didn't like much of what happened after my return to earth, and I prayed many times for relief from the pain, but here is where I am. It's like the story of Jonah. God told him to go to Nineveh and a lot of things had to transpire before he got there, including being devoured by a great fish. His story started in disobedience (which does make it different from mine), but God used his life.

I've also pointed out elsewhere in this book the many trials and hardships of godly people. Would David have been as good a king without his years of struggle? Would Joseph of the Old Testament ever have reached the place of supremacy in Egypt if his brothers hadn't sold him into slavery? The answers are obvious, but we also remind ourselves that God uses empty, cracked, and broken vessels. Paul wrote: "Remember, dear brothers and sisters, that few of you were wise in the world's eyes, or powerful, or wealthy when God called you. Instead, God deliberately chose things the world considers foolish in order to shame those who think they are wise" (1 Corinthians 1:26–27*).

No, I don't rejoice over what happened to me, but I do give thanks that good things have come out of my personal tragedy. Would I be who I am without my suffering? Definitely not. I'm a long way from the person I'd like to be and from the person I used to be, but I do know that my own suffering has made me more open and sensitive to others in their hardships.

The apostle Paul exhorted the Thessalonians to give thanks in all circumstances. That's my goal: Each day to give thanks to God for the life I have now and the doors of ministry he has opened for me. Before my accident in 1989, I could never, never, never have envisioned that God would use such a tragic event to place me where I am today.

In my circumstances, I am grateful to be alive and to be a useful instrument of God.

Holy God, thank you for the life you have given me. Sometimes I wish it were different, but you know who I am and you chose what you wanted me to do or to be. No matter what you do in my life, enable me to thank you in the midst of my circumstances because your loving presence is always with me. Amen.

Confess your sins to each other and pray for each other
so that you may be healed.

—JAMES 5:16[*]

24

BEING STRONG

When Cec attended his mother's funeral, it was naturally a painful time for him. Here is the story in his words:

Mom died quite suddenly, although she was eighty and had been in bad health for a long time. After I flew from Atlanta to Davenport, Iowa, for the funeral, I sat with my three sisters and two brothers. As in many families, Mom had been the family center. My siblings all lived in the same town and they leaned heavily on her.

Mom's former pastor preached the funeral—a man who had known her well—and he spoke of her commitment to Christ and her prayers for the family. My siblings started to cry, really cry, especially two of my sisters. I was seated between them and I hugged both of them.

Throughout the next few days while I was in town, I spent

most of my time hugging, praying, and encouraging my siblings. After all, I was the professional minister. They were so taken up in their grief, they weren't able to focus on my loss, and I understood.

As I sat on the airplane going back to my home in Atlanta and pondered the events of the previous days, I realized what had happened. I had tried to be strong for them. I had tried to shield them and did everything I could to lessen their pain.

But no one had been there for me.

That's not a complaint, because I could have made my feelings known to others. I had old friends in the city. I could have spoken to the pastor. *I didn't allow myself to feel.* I had blocked my feelings so I could focus on theirs.

I had made a choice—unconscious, perhaps—but a choice. I chose to be strong for everybody else. As a pastor, I had been at the bedside of many and I had held grieving people in my arms at their times of loss. I've also been a mourner when I lost friends.

My mistake—and I truly believe it was a mistake—was that I pushed aside *my* need. I came across as strong and comforting, and perhaps I was. What didn't come across was that I also hurt. I had lost my mother just like my siblings had. They faced their grief—openly and without shame.

Because I remained strong, I was the loser. I was the loser because I also didn't want to acknowledge my pain. Again, that wasn't a conscious thought—at least not until later.

I've also seen other people who have had a similar attitude. Maybe like me, they were too busy taking care of others to take care of themselves. Maybe they were too busy being strong.

Those events taught me a powerful lesson and I want to pass it on to others: We don't only have to be strong for others in their loss. Our pain, our grief, our loss is just as real and just as meaningful to us as their feelings are to them. There is no command in the Bible for us to deny, minimize, or ignore our problems. In fact, we cheat others out of the opportunity to minister to us. God's plan is for all of us to bear each other's burdens.

God, forgive me for trying to be strong for others at the cost of denying my pain. You know my weaknesses, my hurts, and my losses. Help me to face them so that I can receive healing from you and live in expectation of the better days ahead. Amen.

We can rejoice, too, when we run into problems and trials, for we know that they are good for us—they help us learn to endure. And endurance develops strength of character in us, and character strengthens our confident expectation of salvation. And this expectation will not disappoint us. For we know how dearly God loves us . . .

—ROMANS 5:3–5[*]

25

DISAPPOINTMENTS TO DIVINE APPOINTMENTS

"Everyone wants an easy ride," he said. I stared at the quad-riplegic, a veteran of the war in Afghanistan. "I had my life figured out. I was going to stay in the service to get my education benefits . . ." He told me about his planned career as a high school football and track coach. "Life sure didn't turn out the way I planned."

As I stared at him, I started to say something to console him, but then his face lit up and he said, "But that disappointment changed my life. I went from disappointment to see my life as a divine appointment."

That story I had to hear.

"I can't teach any sports—not only because of my lack of mobility, but I don't have the physical stamina," he said. "But God opened doors I never knew existed."

He works for a large corporation and his job is to be an advocate for people with disabilities—physical, emotional, and mental. "I didn't know such a position existed and I wouldn't have been fit for it anyway—except for my big D." (His disappointment.)

As I listened to him, I admired his attitude. He told me he had gone from total desperation and turned it into divine aspiration. "I wanted to die. I begged the doctor at the hospital to give me some kind of shot to end it all," he said.

"I understand," I said. "In my case, God took an awful mess and turned it into a message." Aside from trying to be clever with the phrase, I meant something serious and he understood what I was trying to say.

Life had disappointed both of us. My accident and his being shot weren't part of our long-term plans. We expected life to go well with us and to have an easy ride. But neither of us ended up anywhere near what we had expected, wanted, or looked toward.

"I'm a Christian," he said. Like me, he had become a believer at age sixteen. "But if I had known what was going to happen, I wouldn't have signed on to being a Christian." He went on to say, despite that, God had been with him and he had been aware of that reality. The first person who helped him was another soldier who was also a quadriplegic. "He had such a smile on his face and such a spiritual presence about him," the former soldier said. "He was God's messenger to give me hope. Since then I've moved on and grown."

I didn't say much after that. What was there to say? I had expected to comfort him and to make life more meaningful to him. He had shown me, as a living example, that the big D doesn't have to control us. The only thing that we want to control us is the big G—God.

Loving heavenly Father, yes, I want the easy ride—but I know that's not your plan for me. You didn't call me to take easy rides or soft paths. You called me to let my light shine in darkness. And sometimes that light has to shine through my disappointments. Remind me of that. Amen.

[Jesus said,] "If you forgive those who sin against you, your heavenly Father will forgive you. But if you refuse to forgive others, your Father will not forgive your sins."

—MATTHEW 6:14–15*

26

DID YOU EVER MEET HIM?

One of the most frequently asked questions I receive concerns the driver of the truck that hit me. He was a convicted criminal from a nearby prison. He had not been licensed to drive the truck. I've always assumed his inexperience of driving an eighteen-wheeler on a long, narrow bridge is what caused the accident.

My answer is that I never met him, although I've wanted to meet him. I wanted to know how he felt. Did he feel guilty? Did he care? Was he angry at the prison system or life in general?

By the time I had recovered enough from my accident, he had been paroled. I found out he wound up in San Antonio after he got out of jail, but I haven't been able to locate him.

It's not likely that we'll meet, but sometimes I think about him. To me, he's just a faceless man. Although I have his name, I don't know what he looks like or how he feels about the accident or about his own life.

The question about whether I met him also raises another one—although no one actually asks. I think they want to know if I forgive him or if I hold him responsible for what happened.

I don't hold any anger against him, but I certainly think he's responsible. He was driving. The prison officials who asked him to drive may have been even more responsible.

But as I've thought about the question of forgiveness, I remember a lot of bitter words from hurting people. One way people hold on to their hurt and their pain is that they refuse to forgive those who have wounded them. They let the grudges stay deep inside them. They don't want to forgive.

"I don't want him to have the satisfaction of knowing I've forgiven him," one man said about his partner who had cheated him out of almost a million dollars. I didn't argue with the wronged man, but I felt sorry for him. What a heavy burden he carries. Every day he thinks about the wrong done to him. Until he's ready to let it go, that anger stays inside.

And that lack of forgiving also means two other things to me. First, if we don't forgive we don't understand grace. God's grace means that, although we're guilty and deserve punishment, God wipes away our sins. Second, we can't forgive until we know what it's like to be forgiven. Maybe that's why some people hold on to their pain—they don't feel forgiven. I wonder how they feel when they recite the Lord's Prayer asking God to "forgive us our debts [or trespasses] as we forgive . . ."

If they'll ponder those words and truly forgive, their lives will be so much richer.

Loving and always-forgiving God, help me forgive others who have hurt me or wronged me. Remind me that I don't deserve your forgiveness, but you give it anyway. Teach me to let go of the pain and live a fulfilled life. Amen.

And my God will meet all your needs according to his glorious riches in Christ Jesus.

—PHILIPPIANS 4:19[**]

27

HOPE GIVERS

"I'll bet you're glad that driver who hit you was already in prison," one man said to me. That was the first time anyone had talked that way and it shocked me.

I've thought about that, and no, I'm not glad he's in prison. (He's out now.) Too often we don't think about people behind bars. One of the reasons some people are glad is because they don't have to think about them. They're "put away," as I've often heard it said.

I don't mean to argue whether many prisoners deserve their sentence, but I do want to stress that they may be where we can show them the love of Jesus Christ more fully. That may be a time when some of them have hit the bottom and want help.

We've all heard of jailhouse religion, and perhaps one reason is because the prisoners are forced to think and to examine their lives. They're alone. They can't run away from themselves. And that just may be the best opportunity for them to open themselves to God.

Perhaps one of the things we can do is to become the loving arms of hope to those behind prison bars. Everyone isn't suited to do prison ministry, and not all believers want to do it, but we do have a calling to serve others and to be open to them in their need.

By contrast, from a prison cell, Paul wrote a beautiful letter to the Philippians to thank them for their gifts. He called their gifts "a fragrant offering, an acceptable sacrifice, pleasing to God" (Philippians 4:18**). Because they remembered him in his chains and because they provided for him, he added, "My God will meet all your needs . . ."

We all want to be filled with hope, and we often focus on that. Another thing we can do is to become hope givers. Think of those who are incarcerated today, especially those who seriously try to figure out "What's next?" They have a lot of time to pray. They have plenty of time to think and to plan about what happens next. It may be years, even decades, before they get out of prison. A number of people have donated copies of *90 Minutes in Heaven* to prisoners, and a few prisoners have written to thank me for the messages in the book.

I also think of other types of prisons. I was a prisoner for 108 days in the hospital because I couldn't get up to walk. Most of the time I couldn't even get out of bed without help. Although that's not what he meant, I like the words of Isaiah: "The people who walk in darkness will see a great light" (Isaiah 9:2a*). That's the one ministry most of us can do: We can bring light into the darkness. We can open our hearts and stretch out our hands to those who don't know how to help themselves.

In Matthew 25, Jesus talked about the end of the world, and he commended those who visited those in prison, fed the hungry, and visited the sick. Maybe all of us—in some form—can become ministers of hope. Maybe each of us can bring just a little light into the darkness to set prisoners free.

God of all light, please forgive me for thinking mostly about myself, my problems, and my pain. They are important, but I also know that I can offer hope to others and show them light to lead them out of their darkened prisons. Help me, God, to bring them hope. Amen.

Carry each other's burdens, and in this way
you will fulfill the law of Christ.
—GALATIANS 6:2[**]

28
A TOUCH OF PRIDE

At the funeral he sat in the second row with the rest of the family. He stared straight at me as I preached. I knew the family well and his father had been a good friend. Although I had never met Steve, the older son, I recognized him from pictures. During the entire funeral, I saw no show of emotion. His mother and sister wept quietly. Steve's brother didn't cry, but his lips trembled, and I saw the grief etched across his features.

At the end of the funeral, I overheard someone say, "That Steve was so courageous and stoic. He's handling this well, isn't he?"

I resisted the impulse to ask, "Is he?"

I've met people like Steve who don't seem to struggle with their feelings. Earlier we wrote about Cec being the one who hugged his siblings and ignored his own emotions. That situation happens all the time. There's one other factor to look at.

It's what I call a sense of pride—subtle but real. Cec would be the first to admit that was a factor in his situation.

When I talk to most people about their terrible situations, such as the loss of a job, the dissolution of a marriage, or the death of a loved one, they often open up. I've seen strong men—men who never show emotion—fall apart and wail. Once those strong types calm down they start to apologize. I usually stop them.

"You hurt. You feel pain," I like to say. "This is the best way to cope. It's okay to feel it and to express it."

But not everyone does that. Some have their emotions so tightly controlled that they can't express those sad feelings. "I'm doing all right," they say. Or "I'm coping."

They miss out on being nurtured and encouraged and strengthened by others. When the apostle Paul exhorted the Galatians to carry each other's burdens, he meant just that. No matter how heavy the load, when another person is there to share it with us, we become stronger.

When we push aside, ignore, or deny our feelings around other people, we may have a lot of reasons for doing that, but one of them is pride. It's as if to say, "I am absolutely all right. I don't need help."

Some people live by the motto: "It's Jesus and me. If he's with me, I don't need anyone or anything." That's inaccurate.

In fact, the truth is exactly the opposite. When Paul exhorted the Galatians to bear each other's burdens, no one was exempt. Everybody needs someone else.

Jesus sent his disciples out by twos. Paul traveled with Barnabas or Silas, as well as with others. At creation, God said, "It is not good for the man to be alone. I will make a helper suitable for him" (Genesis 2:18**). It was more than someone just to keep Adam from being lonely. Eve was also to be his helper—someone to share life with him. There was no grief or sin at creation, but in time, the couple must have learned to lean on each other. That was God's plan.

We all need other people and that was an invaluable lesson for me to learn. For several months after my accident, I had to depend on others to do everything for me. My family was always there and friends, church members, and sometimes even strangers helped my family to help me.

As I learned, it's not weakness to ask for help, as one man told me. In fact, I told him, it was his pride that stopped him. "We need each other, especially in our troubled times."

God, forgive me when I think it's weak to be vulnerable and needy. Forgive me when I think good Christians ought to be able to handle all their own problems by themselves. Remind me that others can lift me up, give me perspective, and especially, they can offer me hope. Thank you. Amen.

Then Jacob woke up and said, "Surely the Lord is in this place, and I wasn't even aware of it." He was afraid and said, "What an awesome place this is! It is none other than the house of God—the gateway to heaven!"

—Genesis 28:16–17*

29

The New Normal

I read the bumper sticker on the van in front of me: "Life Happens."

How many times have I read that or similar statements? That day, however, long after the van had passed me, I couldn't get those two words out of my mind. Yes, I said to myself, life does happen. Another way to say it is that life changes. All of us have those times when the "happens" drastically changes everything. We can never go back to the old way—the "normal" behavior or circumstances.

What had been normal becomes simply the way life used to be. Because we can't go backward, the best we can do is to learn to accept our life as it is now, move forward, and discover a new kind of normal.

On January 18, 1989, I died because an eighteen-wheeler plunged into my car and killed me. After I returned to earth ninety minutes later, I had to find life again. I had to find what I call a new normal.

Everyone's life doesn't alter drastically as mine did, but all of us have those times when we look at *what was* and compare it with *what is*. Some of us have had to face that a number of times; others have a single experience that is as powerful a line of demarcation as the line between B.C. and A.D.

Because the old way—the old normal—is gone, we have to find a new one. As I was to learn, I could never be the old Don Piper again. Not only had my time in heaven changed me—and that would have been enough—but my physical condition made me a different person. Over the next fifteen years, I underwent thirty-four surgeries. Many physical activities I had taken for granted were no longer possible. My life had been transformed into a different pattern.

Our lives change in many ways. For instance, in the Bible, we read that Jacob ran away from home because of his own wrongdoing and his twin brother, Esau, threatened to kill him. While he was alone and away from home, Jacob saw God in a dream and God promised a future blessing. God had always been with him, but Jacob only then became aware of God's presence, and his life changed.

In the story about Adam and Eve eating the forbidden fruit, the Bible says their eyes were opened and they saw that they were naked. They had always been naked, but then they became aware of their condition (see Genesis 3:6–7) and their lives changed.

For most of us, it's more than an awareness—it's a life-shifting experience—and we can never return to the way life was, even though we may cry out for it.

Part of our happiness depends on accepting the new reality that we are now living. This is how I function now. I can make it the best phase of my life or I can refuse to accept the changes. It's up to me. But this much I can tell anyone: If we accept the new normal, life will be happier and easier.

Dear God, I may not like the things that have changed; I wish my life had not altered. But it has. Remind me that because you love me and are in control of my life, this phase of my life can be as good as or even better than the way life was before. Amen.

I waited patiently for the Lord; he turned to me and heard my cry. He lifted me out of the slimy pit, out of the mud and mire; he set my feet on a rock and gave me a firm place to stand.

—PSALM 40:1–2*

30

CHANGES AND DECISIONS

When life forces a drastic shift of direction, not only have circumstances shifted, but *we have changed* and we make choices—we *have to* make choices because we can't stay the same as we were. As I've thought of how my life altered after my accident, I can point out three distinct differences.

As I've already said, my experience in dying and returning to life changed me—that's the obvious one. No matter how I looked at life after that, my perspective had been transformed. In my case, I was able to see life from an eternal perspective. For example, many things that had seemed extremely important before I went to heaven seem irrelevant now. Everyone's life view may not change like that. In fact, some may feel, at least in the beginning, as if they have lost all eternal perspective. They may become despondent and think nothing matters, or that since life is so uncertain they must live for today and not think of the consequences. But that's temporary. One of the facts about moving into the new normal is that it forces us to take a long-term view of life. We do that almost by default. We see one factor altered and that one thing affects everything else.

Another change in my life was that after my accident, I saw how much I needed other people (not an easy lesson for me). I saw that as a fundamental principle in my life—not just for the time I was in the hospital and for my recuperation. I understood that every human on earth is connected and we need each other to offer love, hope, and connection. I could never go back to my attitude of, "I don't need help."

Finally, and most important, I learned from the forced changes in my life that I couldn't undo anything but I was never alone in my suffering. I could feel sorry for myself (and I did), or I could groan about how terrible my life was (and I did), but through all the ordeals I learned that God heard my cries for help. No matter how desperate I felt or how sick, God was with me. I knew he would lift me out of the pit of life—eventually—and he did.

Dear caring God, at times I wondered when you would respond to my cries. Many times I've grown impatient. But I've learned that as I adjust to a new life, a new normal, you have heard me and you are preparing to set my feet on a solid rock. For this, I thank you. Amen.

*He has given me a new song to sing, a hymn of praise to
our God. Many will see what he has done and be
astounded. They will put their trust in the Lord.*

—Psalm 40:3[*]

31

ADDED VALUE

George Arnold is nearly eighty years old. When he was
fifty, he had just about everything he wanted in life: a
loving wife, children, an excellent income, and a beautiful
house near the mountains. He felt he had just about everything
going for him.

Then his wife died when he was sixty. The next year, one of
his daughters died in a car accident. By the time he was seventy, he learned that the company for which he had worked for
forty-one years had gone bankrupt. The president had either
embezzled or misused funds and his retirement income was
gone.

Years later, George told me that although he missed his wife
and child, the losses in his life had made him a better person.

He spoke about his sheltered, self-centered life. But when everything crashed, he discovered what was really important in his life. George had been a Christian since childhood, but after his losses, Christianity took on a new depth and stronger meaning.

His story isn't all that different from thousands of others. When we leave the old normal—the old ways—we always leave only because we're forced to do so. As a result, our attitudes change. Our values alter. We see people and events differently. If we learn well, we become stronger, wiser, and more mature in our relationships. If we don't learn well, we keep repeating old thinking and behaviors in an attempt to undo or relive the past.

Most of us go through one or several life-shattering experiences. They may be glorious, joyful, and positive, like my time in heaven; they may be painful, traumatic, and negative like the 108 days I spent in the hospital.

On the positive side, some have gotten married, had their first baby, landed their dream job, or inherited a large amount of money. Those kinds of changes normally reflect a joyous movement to a new normal. Life may not be quite as blessed as the dreams we had before entering into those relationships, but it's still good.

Not many people need encouragement to enjoy being happy but they surely need help when negative changes happen. Some of us have gone through a divorce, have been down-sized, have been rejected by a parent or a child, or have lost a loved one.

No matter what the situation, we are no longer the same individuals we were before that crucial moment of change.

"What do I do now?" After they pour out their pain, that's one of the questions they ask. Or sometimes, they know they're stuck and unable to move ahead, so they ask me, "How do I get on with my life?"

One thing has to be totally clear before we can adjust and move into a new way of life: We must be convinced that we can *never* go back to the way life used to be. We may struggle, cry, pray, or yearn to have life just the way it was, but we can't return to what no longer exists.

Too often most of us have heard people in the midst of their pain cry out, "I just want my life to be the way it used to be."

That won't happen.

There is no turning back or going back. We have to adjust. We have to find a new kind of normalcy. One of the reasons I am on the road so much is because I want to bring joyful expectation to others. I want people to see that because life is bad now doesn't mean life must remain unbearable. I want to help others find the way, regain their balance, and learn to enjoy life to the fullest, even after everything has drastically and unalterably changed.

The most important point I want to make is this: Life never stays constant. And every serious change means we must leave old ways behind and accept new paths (the new normal), often with added value in our lives. Even when we know we're going in the right direction, the adjustment is always uncomfortable, and it's usually difficult.

I am not the same man I was before the accident. I'm not the same man I was two years after the accident. I constantly change because my life refuses to become static. For example, when my book *90 Minutes in Heaven* came off the press in October 2004, I had no way to know how my life would be altered forever. I had no way to see into the future and realize that God would use me to bring hope and encouragement to people around the world. But it happened.

God has truly "given me a new song to sing," and I'm amazed at the platform I have from which I can speak to people as they "put their trust in the Lord." I didn't ask for the added value, but I embrace it because that's part of God's loving plan for me—for now—for this phase of my new normal.

Wise God, when I was at my lowest point, I could never have dreamed or imagined what my life would be or could be. Remind me that you are able to do far beyond anything I can expect or imagine. Amen.

When Jacob awoke from his sleep, he thought, "Sure the
Lord is in this place, and I was not aware of it."
—Genesis 28:16***

32

DIVINE APPOINTMENTS

I flew to Sweden in 2005 to speak to people all over that country. My interpreter was Joel, who worked with Gospel Media. One evening after I finished a speaking engagement at a conference, Joel left the van at the top of a steep hill, and we walked down the hill to a restaurant. After we ate, we started to walk back up the hill.

"I know you have trouble with steps," Joel said. "Why don't you wait here and I'll go up and get the van and drive down here to pick you up?"

I refused. I wasn't being gallant. I thought I could make it easily enough and hadn't realized the steepness of the hill. Going down had been easy, but now it was also quite dark so I couldn't see how far away the van was parked.

"You might stumble in the dark," Joel persisted, but I

remained adamant. We started upward. After a few hundred yards, I realized the walk was extremely steep, more like walking up a mountain. "I'll make it," I said and wondered if I had made a wise decision.

Just then a large, blue-eyed blond man raced up to us. In broken English he said, "Reverend Piper, my name is Sven."

"Hello," I said and stuck out my hand to shake his. The man began to cry.

"What's the matter?" I asked.

Sven was so agitated, he couldn't speak in English so Joel translated. Sven said his wife had left him only that morning. She said she was through with him and the marriage and left.

He and his wife had planned to attend the conference together. He decided to come alone and hoped he could find answers—or at least some peace. He said he had sat in the church and listened. "But no peace came. I felt totally alone and that no one else cared," he said through Joel. Several times he mentioned how much he loved his wife and didn't want the marriage to end.

"If God can resuscitate a dead guy in a red car," I said, "he can put your marriage back together again."

"Yes, I want my marriage put back together."

I sensed that the breakup hadn't been sudden, so I asked, "Has this been going on for a long time?"

"Yes, but lately it has gotten extremely bad."

We talked a few minutes as we continued up the hill. I

slowed down because it was hard to walk that incline. After I had listened to his story and offered advice, I said, "I'm leaving in the morning, but there is something I can do tonight. I'm going to pray for you right now."

"Yes, I would like that."

"Joel lives here and he'll try to get you some help through the local church. Right now, we're going to commit this broken relationship to God."

The three of us linked arms and prayed. Afterward Sven embraced me—and I knew he wasn't the kind of man who did that easily. As we stood together on the side of the road, it seemed as if Sven couldn't thank me enough.

Finally, Joel and I left Sven and finished our slow trudge up the hill. Just before we reached the top, Joel said, "You almost didn't walk up the road. If you had taken my suggestion, we wouldn't have met Sven."

"That's right."

"But you wanted to take the steps," Joel said almost to himself, "and if we had taken the van we wouldn't have met Sven, and he needed us."

As I listened, I thought, that's a divine appointment. God sends people my way when I have no warning. I'm not the only one. If we stay open to God, all of us have such divine appointments.

God is here. God is everywhere. We say those words, but once in a while we have a kind of Sven experience. We're in the right place and we have a divine appointment. We're up-lifted and we help another person in the process. That's a divine appointment.

Lord God, help me realize that not only are you here at every moment, but you have servants everywhere to send to me in my moments of need. You have divine appointments set up for me when I need you most, like meeting Sven in a moment of need. Thank you for that assurance. Amen.

*[Jesus said,] ". . . For [God] gives his sunlight
to both the evil and the good, and he sends rain
on the just and on the unjust, too."*

—MATTHEW 5:45[*]

33

"BUT WHY? WHY? WHY?"

"I've lost my daughter," the woman said as soon as she had introduced herself to me on the phone. "She accidentally overdosed on prescription medication. Why? Why would that happen?"

Whether it was accidental or intentional wasn't the issue. The daughter was dead and the mother needed comfort in her grief.

"She's been a believer for years," she added.

As I listened, I realized the mother not only felt a terrible sense of loss but one of guilt. "I failed her in some way," the woman said again and again and filled her story with if-only statements: "*If only* I had checked on my daughter earlier in the day." "*If only* I had watched more carefully." "*If only* I had made sure she took only the required dosage each time."

I tried to say all the positive things I could think of to comfort her. More than once, I said, "If she was a believer, she's at peace. She's with the Lord right now."

Those words brought some comfort, but the woman still seemed troubled.

"But why? Why? Why? Why did she die from an overdose?"

"I don't know," I said, and that was a totally honest answer. I've heard the question hundreds of times. Other distraught people have gone through a variety of tragedies and many ask why. "Why did I lose my job?" "Why did I develop a debilitating disease?" Or the question can be as simple as the teenaged girl who never gets a date and asks, "Why don't boys like me?"

I don't know. None of us know. That's the simplest answer to such questions. However, I can't just drop it there. When people are in pain, their period of grief isn't the time to reason with them. They often ask the why question, but they really want God to answer a different one, "Do you love me, God? Do you care?"

Every one of us needs to find ways to make sense out of life. And when life goes out of control—meaning our personal control—we're left confused and with great loss. "How can this be?"

The immediate reaction of most of us is, "What did I do wrong? How did I fail?"

Or I think about the church secretary who told me about a family in her church. "They have been the most faithful givers and doers in our congregation."

Yet they suffered one serious illness after another. "They're such good Christians," she said. "They don't deserve such bad things."

I hear that a lot. It implies that people usually deserve their problems.

As I listened, I agreed: They didn't deserve it.

I didn't deserve my accident.

People often conclude that bad things happen only when people do something wrong. They sin and God punishes them. It's the simplistic thinking that says, "If something goes wrong, I have to keep searching until I find the reason and then all will be well."

But will it?

Probably not.

We all have problems. We all have questions that have no answers. That's how life works and it's sometimes beyond our understanding. The lack of answers makes it even more difficult for believers. We feel there must be an explanation and we'll have no peace unless we know the reason. So we constantly cry out, "Why, God? Why?" Or if we can't figure out the answer, we try to console ourselves and mumble, "Someday we'll know the reason."

Maybe. Maybe not.

What I did say to that grieving mother and what I can say to any others who seem overwhelmed with grief and unable to understand is this: "God loves you. God cares about your pain. The suffering you feel is genuine and the loving God of creation wants to heal your grief. There is no insurance against problems or heartaches in this life."

Even now, I could wallow in the why question about my accident, but none of the answers I could come up with would satisfy me.

Instead of "Why me, God?" isn't it better to ask, "How, God? How do I feel your comfort? How do I draw close? How can I move beyond my pain?" As we start to ask the right questions, we move closer to the correct answers.

God of comfort, I don't understand the troubles in my life or the losses I've suffered. Sometimes I get discouraged over such things. Help me to reach out toward your ever-loving arms that want to enfold me and give me comfort in the midst of my pain. Amen.

And I am sure that God, who began the good work within you, will continue his work until it is finally finished on that day when Christ Jesus comes back again.

—Philippians 1:6*

34
God's Plan for My Life

"God has a plan for your life," the pastor said. The first time I heard those words, I listened closely. Perhaps I also listened carefully the second and third times as well. Eventually, I had heard that phrase so often I didn't pay much attention.

What does it mean to say that God has a plan for us? That God has a plan for me personally? And yet we do want to believe that. When tragedies occur, we sometimes become desperate to hang on to those words

"God has a plan for you, Don Piper, even though you're in the hospital, living in constant pain, and you don't know if you'll survive." I'm glad no one said those words to me while I was in the hospital or even during the first months of my recuperation when I was home but unable to walk or do anything for myself. It would not have been the message I wanted to hear.

I wonder how easily people in pain would welcome these words: "God has a plan for you, even though you're dying of cancer." "God has a plan for you, even though you used to earn $200,000 a year and now you have no job and no insurance."

Even though it's true, that's not the time most people want to hear those words. God does have a plan for us, for each of us. Paul wrote to the Philippians that God had begun a good work in their lives and assured them that God wouldn't stop until Jesus returned. He also wrote to the Ephesians, "For we are God's masterpiece. He has created us anew in Christ Jesus, so that we can do the good things he planned for us long ago" (Ephesians 2:10*).

When all goes well, we have no difficulty in believing those words. We like to hear them and they assure us of God's loving presence. But when tragedy or pain rules, we wonder. We question. We don't see that divine plan in action, or maybe we've misunderstood what the apostle meant.

If we assume God plans for our lives to be easy, carefree, and only prosperous, we've misunderstood many of the words of the Bible. In the years since my accident, I've come to believe that we *need* hardship. If everything went well, we wouldn't need to cry to God. We wouldn't call out for deliverance. We'd do it ourselves. We wouldn't need a Savior.

I don't understand God's plan for anyone else's life, and not even my own, but I do know it means that when the hard times come, in response I grow in my dependence on God. No matter what happens, God is still my helper and my resource. God is the one to whom I cry out, "Help me, Lord."

We face the same issues and traumas of people who have no knowledge of him. The difference is that we have spiritual resources. We have a compassionate, caring God who embraces us and gives us peace while storms rage around us.

Yes, God does have a plan, and yes, God will continue to work out that plan in our lives until Jesus returns to earth or we go to heaven to meet him. That's the assurance any of us can offer to each other.

Dear loving God, thank you that you truly have a plan for my life. I'm not some afterthought, because you've always loved me. You've always had a design for my life so that I would become your masterpiece. Because you assure me of your plan, you also assure me of your love. Thank you. Amen.

*"Comfort, comfort my people," says your God.
"Speak tenderly to Jerusalem. Tell her that her
sad days are gone and that her sins are pardoned.
Yes, the Lord has punished her in full for all her sins."*

—ISAIAH 40:1–2[*]

35

COMFORT FROM THE PAIN

Tammy from Portland e-mailed me, "Mom became a believer." Tammy went on to say that only a short time before she died, her mother read *90 Minutes in Heaven* and found great comfort.

Tammy said the last weeks of her mother's life were extremely painful. She loved her mother deeply and she also found comfort as she read about heaven and knew her mother was in a place of peace.

I'm so grateful that I could bring this woman and her mother hope and comfort. God has enabled me to share my personal experience with others so they can look forward to heaven themselves. But perhaps even more important for some of them is that they find peace when they think about their loved ones. When I try to put my experience into words, their responses help me know it's the message they need.

Tammy also asked me to pray that the thought of her mother in heaven would become more real to her each day and that it would continue to bring her and her family comfort.

As I pondered those words, I realized Tammy struggled as many do. She wanted to remember her mother's love and life, but she also needed comfort in her pain.

And the Bible does offer comfort and encouragement to us. For example, one of the most powerful statements in the Bible about comfort comes from Isaiah, Chapter 40. The Jews had been sent into exile for seventy years. They had suffered every imaginable hardship. In their case, it was punishment because they had failed God, refused to listen to the prophets, and continued to sin. God warned them again and again, and after years of warning, the judgment fell. God punished them severely and their enemies overcame them, took them into a foreign land, and killed many of them. That might have been the end of most nations and races, but the loving, compassionate God sent word through the prophet Isaiah to comfort the chosen people. "Speak tenderly to Jerusalem," he said.

God wanted them to know they had paid for their sins and had received forgiveness. This isn't to imply that every person who has a loss or goes through suffering is being punished by God. It's really a message of contrast to show the grace of God.

If God would pardon the people of Israel after their constant rebellion and send words of comfort to them, what does that say to us today? What does that say to people who haven't been in utter rebellion but are overwhelmed with problems?

The message is the same: God cares. God offers comfort. We need to understand that if God embraced the Jews after all their rebellion, how much more would God extend loving comfort to people who are in pain and who feel loss?

At the end of Chapter 40 in Isaiah, God promises, "But those who hope in the Lord will renew their strength. They will soar on wings like eagles; they will run and not grow weary, they will walk and not be faint" (Verse 31[**]).

Dear God of comfort, thank you for your extended hand that offers me comfort in my times of discouragement. Thank you that you care even when I don't feel your closeness or compassion. And thank you that I can find renewed strength from you. Amen.

And we know that God causes everything
to work together for the good of those who love God
and are called according to his purpose for them.

—ROMANS 8:28[*]

36

DEEPER WELLS

The first time I met Sam in an Atlanta hospital, the fifteen-year-old boy was in bad shape. He and his friend had been running Jet Skis on a lake. They had been running beside each other when his leg was caught between the two skis and was almost severed. Exacerbating the situation was that the lake wasn't clean. Sam not only had a massive open wound, but he was in danger of severe infection. When they got him to the hospital, they weren't sure they could save his leg. They did save the leg but he wore a fixator[1] on it.

When I met him, Sam was depressed. I talked to him for a long time, because I had worn a fixator on my leg for months.

---

[1] A fixator is an immobilization device used to hold rods and pins through fractured bones. See *90 Minutes in Heaven*.

I knew the pain he was going through. He listened, but I had no idea if my words meant anything to him.

When I told him about my own situation, I showed him pictures of my leg in a fixator and then I said, "My well is a lot deeper than it used to be."

As I spoke those words, I realized how true they were. They were true for me and they were true for countless others. Until we've been knocked down, had our hearts broken, or suffered deep grief, we can't relate to people like Sam. I reflected on my own role as a pastor and the people I had visited in the hospital throughout those years.

Yes, I thought, I said words to encourage them, patted them on the back, and tried to be available when they needed me. I did care and I wanted to comfort them. After more than thirty surgeries, however, I realized that I related to people differently. It wasn't so much that my words changed, but *I* had changed.

"My well is deeper," I said. "I have more depth from which to draw living water." I had held the hands of others before and prayed, and I gave as much of myself as I knew how. I gave them what I had to offer, but since those days, I know I have much more of myself to give.

There is no substitute for pain, suffering, and heartaches to deepen our wells of understanding. That's why Paul's words carry so much meaning. When tragedy falls, we can spend the rest of our lives in regret—and many do—or we can use our misfortunes to help others.

About a year after I first met Sam, his mother e-mailed me to say that he had been in the orthopedic doctor's office for a checkup. While he waited, he saw a young girl with a fixator on her leg. Sam got up and walked over to the girl. He sat down beside her. "I know you hate that and the pain is awful," he said. "I know. I had one of them on my leg for months."

Sam's mother listened as Sam brought comfort and encouragement to the young girl. "I want you to know that this has come full circle," Sam's mother wrote. "My son is doing for others the kind of thing you did for him." At the end of her e-mail, she added, "There were many times we never thought we'd get this far."

When those things happen, we see God's grace at work. We become divine instruments to ease the pain and hardship of others. But first, we have to get outside of ourselves and move beyond our own pain. We need to see the circumstances that we've gone through as meaningful. Then we can understand how to relate to others.

When we move outside of our own troubles, we not only help others, but we help ourselves. That's when we recognize the truth of Paul's words—that everything in the lives of believers works together for good. It's because we have become wounded healers.

Maybe that's what "deeper wells" truly means. We draw from hidden, previously unknown places in our lives. As we draw from our wells, we give sustenance to others. We can share the deeper water only if we have it within our wells. But that deeper water makes us more grateful and thankful for God's presence in our lives.

I know that's true for me. I want my well to go even deeper.

Lord Jesus, please help me. So many times in my life I've grumbled and complained about my hardships. They're very real to me, but I also know you want to deepen my well and want me to draw from subterranean levels. You want me to share some of the living water with others in need. Give me the strength and the desire to do that. Amen.

Dear friends, don't be surprised at the fiery trials you are going through, as if something strange were happening to you. Instead, be very glad—because these trials will make you partners with Christ in his suffering, and afterward you will have the wonderful joy of sharing his glory when it is displayed to all the world.

—I PETER 4:12–13*

37

A BUMPY RIDE

In a 1950 film called *All About Eve*, Bette Davis says, "Fasten your seat belts; it's going to be a bumpy ride." That set up the storyline for a big, dramatic scene. But aren't those words just as indicative of life? We all have what some refer to as the IBs—the inevitable bumps.

So many times we've heard people say, "I went through bad times and now I need to get on with my life." That's good, but it's not enough. Our next step beyond doing something for ourselves is to help others get on with the rest of their lives.

For example, one of the things I like about mutual-help

groups such as Alcoholics Anonymous or Narcotics Anonymous is that no one needs to explain what it feels like to be drunk or to be sober and wish you were drunk. No one needs to tell a member of NA what it means to focus the entire day on finding a fix. No one needs to be told the feeling of being useless and filled with self-hatred.

The biggest benefit of such groups is that they recognize that the members know the problems faced by the newly clean or sober. They also know all the excuses so they won't allow new members to feel sorry for themselves.

For instance, Jane and James used to lead an AA group at a church where Cec was the pastor. "My mission is to help others get on with their lives," James often said.

They knew their mission and they were saddened at the failures of some. But they were able to rejoice in those who succeeded in sobriety. They stayed at that ministry for more than twenty years.

I also think of people in churches who go to other countries on short-term missions. Whether they go to Honduras or Fiji, I've never met anyone who has come back and said, "That was the worst thing I ever did in my life." Instead, when they return they say, "I feel more blessed than the people I went to bless."

They believe they truly went on a mission—and it is a mission because it's a journey with a purpose. They go to build houses, to repair damaged school buildings or to bring medical assistance. What they do isn't as important as the fact that they go, and they see people in need. They visit people without some of the basics we take for granted. The people they help always have far worse problems than they do.

That's when many of them begin to understand the purpose behind the IBs of life. As they look on others who have suffered, and often have suffered a long time, their own bumpy ride seems much smoother. One woman said, "My problems seemed so petty when I visited southern Mississippi after Hurricane Katrina. The day before I went there, I complained in a restaurant when I had to wait twenty minutes for my food. In Mississippi I met people who didn't have a stove on which to cook or a table at which to sit."

Life has bumps for all of us. One way to learn to put our bumps into perspective is to look around us. As we see others with bigger bumps in their roads than we have, it makes us realize how much we have and how thankful we need to be.

When the apostle Peter urged people not to be surprised at their ordeals, he was, of course, referring primarily to persecution because of their faithful witness to Jesus Christ. Even so, this principle is true whenever our lives seem to hit bad, bumpy spots. He wrote about being partners with Christ, and we are. We become partners when we move beyond our pain and offer a healing hand to others.

God, it's easy for me to focus on the bumps, detours, and un-expected curves in my life. Instead, help me learn from them and focus on using my experience to make it easier on others as they travel down their own path. Amen.

[Jesus said,] "Ask and it will be given to you; seek and you will find; knock and the door will be opened to you."

—MATTHEW 7:7**

38
IT'S A PROCESS

Many people want formulas and pat answers to make things happen right now. They want prayers they can repeat so that everything turns out exactly right. But most of life doesn't work that way. Most of the obstacles we encounter in life involve a process to overcome. They take time to work through and it takes time for us to change our attitude and our behavior.

At one time I was the sales manager for a TV station, and our division sold ads. Sometimes I'd come into the office and see seven or eight salespeople at their desks. One day I called the sales force together and said, "We have a good product. We know it works. We've been to all the training sessions and we know what to do. But it's highly unlikely that if we sit here in the office someone is going to come to the front door of this television station and ask, 'Would it be okay if we bought some advertisement time on your station?'" I pointed out that if we wanted to sell ads, we had to go out and meet the people where they were. "You have to knock on doors, and make calls; you have to get out there." I ended by saying, "I'm not telling you anything you don't know, but knowing how to sell does nothing until you get out there and act."

That example reminds me that we frequently encounter people who want to change. They're unhappy with the situations in their lives but they don't seem to want to do anything to change. They want the miracles to come to them. Life doesn't work that way. If we want to turn the corner on our situation, we have to do something. And that means we have to be responsible. People may show sympathy for our problems and pain, but it's *our* lives and *our* predicaments. My advice: Do anything reasonable to get past the problem. Go to therapy. Ask friends for help.

When people come to my meetings, many of them want answers. They seek encouragement, and my messages of hope often give them a handle for their own desperate situations. Often they pour out their stories to me—and some of them are truly heartbreaking. One man told me about his serious accident while driving a truck. It took months for his physical recovery, but in the process he had alienated his children and angered his wife. He wanted his life to come back together for him.

"I understand completely," I said. "I'm not even going to say you weren't entitled to be that way. Did you deserve what happened to you? No, I don't think you did. But now that you know that you've got the rest of your life in front of you, you need to figure out how to do this. You have to make changes yourself."

"I sure do," he admitted.

"That's a start, but it's just a start. Don't think you'll walk out of here and discover you've gotten over this hump. This is the *start* of getting over the obstacle. And you have to be realistic and remind yourself: This is a process. It's not magic, it's not a pill to ingest. It takes time."

As we talked, I also told him, "There were times when I was so sick that they had to give me an injection or pill to make me feel better, but eventually the effects wore off. I had to learn to handle the pain as I got better. Injections take care of the immediate pain, but they're not what we need for the long haul."

I often point out that unless we take action, our sense of hopelessness can become permanent. I've met too many people who live in a permanent state of depression, paralysis, heartbreak, difficulty, anger, and hostility.

I know of only one way to start the inner-healing process, and Jesus said it: Ask, seek, and knock. It starts with our doing something. The New Living Translation makes it clear that Jesus used a verb tense that means to ask and to continue asking. "For everyone who asks, receives. Everyone who seeks, finds. And the door is opened to everyone who knocks" (Matthew 7:8*).

Heavenly Father, please remind me that you've told me to ask and to continue asking, seeking, and knocking. You've promised that if I do what I can, you do what you can—and your resources are unlimited. Thank you that you care enough to give me hope in the midst of my pain and discouragement. Amen.

*God is love, and all who live in love live in God, and God
lives in them. And as we live in God, our love grows more
perfect . . . We love each other as a result of his loving us first.*

—1 JOHN 4:16B–17, 19*

39

ARTIFICIAL INTIMACY

Why do people go to meeting places on the Internet such as myspace.com? It's tagged, "A place for friends." Why are Internet dating services so popular? The answer seems fairly obvious: Those sites reach lonely people. Some are desperate to connect with other human beings, or even just one other person. One thing about the Internet is that it seems to make it easy for people to open up to a screen and type in the most intimate things about themselves.

I've often sat on the plane for four or five hours while someone opened up to me and told me intimate details, often horrible stories that they wouldn't have told anyone else. They needed to open up and unburden themselves and I was available.

Maybe confiding in a stranger on the Internet or the person next to us on a plane is all right because it's safe—safe in the sense that we're sharing intimate details but we're not really close to the person so it is somewhat anonymous. It's not real intimacy, but it's a kind of artificial closeness that helps to ease any loneliness and emptiness in our lives.

"You know, I was seven years old when my father raped me," one woman said to me on a flight from Denver to Dallas. "I've never really recovered from this and I hate men." When she found out I was a preacher she said, "When I hear the words 'Our Father which art in heaven,' they enrage me."

Almost every day I receive e-mails from individuals who pour out their sad, pitiful tales before they add, "I don't know why I'm saying this to you," or "We don't even know each other but I feel safe in telling you this," or "I've read your book and I sense I can trust you."

I think of a time when I was a pastor. A woman sat in my office and told me of the countless sexual affairs she had had during the past nine years. "I'm single and I only go out with single men, so we don't hurt anyone," she said at first to justify her actions. When I pushed her to explain why she had had so many sexual affairs, she broke down and cried. "I want to be loved, I want to be held and cared for, but I have to settle for sex."

She didn't have the right answer, but she knew the problem. Like many others, she wanted intimacy. She wanted to connect and to feel loved. She wanted emotional response and to feel cared about by another human being.

Because I meet so many people in brief encounters, there isn't much I can do on the spot. I listen; I pray for them; I suggest they talk to pastors or counselors.

I wish I could nudge or even push them to genuine intimacy. I want them to love and to feel loved. I want them to know they're not alone in this world. God loves them. They've heard that message, but they haven't always been able to receive it. I wish I could make every person I meet feel loved and wanted by God. For it is only as we know we're loved by God that we're able to be open to true intimacy and not settle for temporary or surface relationships.

Lord Jesus, as I child I used to sing "Jesus Loves Me." I still know all the words, but now I need to know the meaning. Help me to experience your love. Help me to find honest intimacy and connections with others so that I can live a healthier life. Amen.

I . . . hope that I will never do anything
that causes me shame, but that I will always be bold
for Christ . . . and that my life will always honor Christ,
whether I live or I die.

—PHILIPPIANS 41:20–21*

40

"OUR PASTOR DIED"

"We need you to come to our church."

The invitation came by e-mail from a deacon in a church in Arizona. One of his church members had visited friends in Texas and had heard me speak.

The pastor of the church was killed in a car wreck. Although it had happened almost a month earlier, the people had loved the man and they felt disoriented, disjointed, and still reeled from the emotional blow. The church had an interim who tried to bring healing, but so far nothing had worked.

"Could you come to talk to our church? We need encouragement," the man said.

I accepted the invitation. I realized that they really wanted a living pastor to tell them what had happened to their dead pastor. That was the kind of encouragement I could give them.

The people displayed a wide range of emotions but I tried to focus my message on the most obvious ones. At first, no one was willing to say it aloud, but some questioned whether the pastor's death was God's punishment. "Maybe God is punishing us," someone finally said.

"God is sovereign and can do anything," I said. "You loved the man and he led you spiritually. So here's a question: Why would the Lord punish all of you for a sin done by your leader? Or if your pastor wasn't punished for his sin, it must have been someone in the congregation. Does it seem reasonable that God would take your leader because one or two people have hidden sins? Wouldn't God have left him here to combat the evil within this church?"

As absurd as all of that may sound, I know that when people face the loss of someone they love very much, logic doesn't always prevail. They focus on their loss and can't always see beyond that reality.

They wanted explanations and I had to tell them, "Sometimes there are no explanations. Sometimes we have to trust God's wisdom and timing, despite all the sorrow we face."

I explained that some might have thought God was punishing me when I died, and sent me back to give me another chance. "I was certainly unaware of any sin in my life," I said. "I wasn't running from God. In fact, I had just left a pastors' retreat and planned to preach that night."

I can't explain why some people die in horrible accidents and others don't. I don't know why some good people die young and some wicked people live to be ninety. If we focus only on such events, we lose our perspective.

The proper perspective is that God loves us and is with us, even during the worst of times. There is an old story about the discouraged father who cried out to a pastor, "Where was God when my son died?" The minister said, "The same place he was when his own son died."

God *is* with us—all the time. We can focus on tragedy and ask, "Where was God?" Or we can say, "God, this tragedy hurts. I'm in pain. Help me." Those are the prayers God wants to hear.

When I spoke to the congregation in Arizona, I realized I hadn't said anything that others hadn't already said. But I added one more thing: "Do you think your pastor is sitting at the gate of heaven right now crying because he's not here with you?"

"No, I think he's rejoicing in the presence of the Lord," someone said.

"Absolutely right. So you don't need to weep for him. Weep for your loss, cry because you miss him, but don't weep for him."

I saw several smiles from people who had been crying. I believe the healing had begun.

Gracious God, sometimes I hurt and my situation is all I can think about because the hurt is so deep. Remind me that you are here, right now, ready to encourage me and to lift my spirits. Thank you. Amen.

He [Jesus] withdrew about a stone's throw beyond them,
knelt down and prayed, "Father, if you are willing, take
this cup from me; yet not my will, but yours be done."

—LUKE 22:41–42**

41

SANCTIFIED COMMON SENSE

What does it mean to "find" the will of God? God's will isn't lost and it's not some secret hidden code we have to learn. We don't have to beg God to show us.

I have a theory: When people tell me they begged for God to display his will, it usually means they already know, but they don't want to accept it. It's almost as if they think that if they pray long enough they'll get a different answer. Perhaps they're afraid that if they fully surrender themselves, they'll end up as missionaries in a foreign land or do something they hate doing. They're afraid that God would create people and endow them with individual gifts and then give them jobs they hate or aren't suited to do. That doesn't make sense to me.

I believe God guides us into jobs and careers where we can

discover fulfillment and joy in what we do. For instance, at a New York hotel, I observed a doorman who had held his job for twenty-five years.

"I love doing this. I meet so many wonderful people." He also said he could hardly wait to get to work in the mornings. He was a believer and he felt this was his way to serve God. He didn't think about being a preacher or making a big impression on other lives. He had a job he loved and met people he enjoyed.

I wish every believer was like that man. Christians need something that I call "sanctified common sense." If it doesn't look right, it doesn't smell right, and if it doesn't feel right, it's probably not right. I often joke that God doesn't call blind women to be taxi drivers.

Sanctified common sense means knowing that God loves each of us and gives us specific abilities. We all have some things we do well and some things we don't do well. If we accept what we do well, serve God in that capacity, and keep trying to get better at what we can do, that honors God.

For example, two of us are responsible for this book. I do most of the public speaking and share my insights and experiences with Cec, who then does most of the writing. We call it collaboration, and both of us like that. Both of us feel we're maximizing our abilities.

It's more than maximizing our abilities. When we use our sanctified common sense, we enjoy life more. We help others and we're sensitive to the needs around us. If we have a solid, enjoyable life, it prepares us for the life ahead. We have given ourselves to what God equipped us to do and that prepares us with the right attitude to get into heaven and enjoy the awe of living in his presence.

As I think along that line, I'm reminded of a story Jesus told about three servants put in charge of their master's house. To the faithful, the master said, "Well done, good and faithful servant! . . . Come and share your master's happiness!'" (Matthew 25:21**). The faithful servants received a reward because they did what was right. They did it, not because someone watched over them, but because they put to use their sanctified common sense.

That's all God asks of us. Do what we can do and don't focus on what we can't do. Just before his death, Jesus knew what God the Father wanted him to do. God wanted him to die on a cross. He asked God to release him. Jesus knew the divine will, and that was never the question for him. But he was a human being and he knew the pain and the torture he would have to endure. He closed by praying: " . . . Yet not my will but yours be done" (Luke 22:42**). He prayed for God to deliver him, but he knew, he always had known, the suffering that lay before him. He didn't want torture, but he didn't run away.

Discovering the will of God is a crucial thing, and some of these steps lead us there: prayer, seeking counsel, and especially sanctified common sense. The will of God isn't hidden like eggs at Easter. God will only reveal to us what we're ready to know and to obey.

We may have to pray earnestly, but God will show us. However, if we're not looking, we won't find God's path for us. The more convinced we are that God truly loves us and wants only good in our lives, the more readily we accept God's will. If we pray, as Jesus did, "Yet not my will, but yours be done," the easier it is to surrender joyfully.

God, help me not be afraid to obey. Help me to be so filled with your love that I'll know you want only good things for me. Remind me as often as necessary that you also work through my sanctified common sense. Amen.

. . . Mary . . . sat at the Lord's feet listening to what he said. But Martha was distracted by all the preparations that had to be made. She came to him and asked, "Lord, don't you care that my sister has left me to do the work by myself?" . . . "Martha, Martha," the Lord answered, "you are worried and upset about many things, but only one thing is needed. Mary has chosen what is better . . ."

—LUKE 10:39–42[**]

42

LITTLE THINGS THAT DON'T MATTER

Earlier I referred to an e-mail from a woman who had cancer. She shared with me that everything she went through made her stronger and helped her realize what is important to her. "What does matter to me is my relationship with our Lord, reaching others for him, and of course, my family; other things of this earth pale in comparison."

As I read those words, I realized how true they were and how important. In my own life, on the day of my accident, I had a number of things on my mind and all of them seemed important. I had worked on a message to preach that night at our church. I planned to work on it again before I delivered it. After all these years, I don't remember all the little problems that went through my mind, but I do know this much: They were small issues.

Before that particular day finished, surviving was what mattered. My wife, Eva, teaches school and, like every teacher, she had faced a lot of problems; however, when she heard about my accident, those concerns vanished. I don't want to imply that we ignore or push away the minor things. I do want to emphasize that we need to rethink the big issues and the petty ones. Too often we focus on things that have little or no significance in the long run.

So often in life, the things that clamor the loudest for our attention may be the most insignificant. We used to hear the phrase *the tyranny of the urgent*, and it's still true. Too often we respond to the loudest noise or the angriest voice when we'd do better if we focused on the important issues that confront us.

But our lives change when we're overwhelmed with cancer, divorce, bankruptcy, or a long-term illness. Then we say, "I will never be the same person I was before." We're never the same after a major event disrupts our lives.

No one wants those traumas and hardships and certainly none of us wants to go through such painful events a second time. In retrospect, however, we look back and realize that not only are we stronger for having undergone such a terrible time, but if we've truly grown, we also admit that we don't want to be the way we were before. We're different now and we might even like our new life better.

God, I know I fight against changes, especially the big ones. I don't like my world to be disrupted. But help me to realize that it's in just those dreadful moments when you come to my aid. Enable me to look at such past events and to thank you for being with me during those times. Amen.

Thereafter, Hagar referred to the Lord, who had spoken to her, "as the God who sees me," for she said, "I have seen the One who sees me!"

—GENESIS 16:13*

43

NEW MARKERS

Circumstances change and we can't do things the way we did before. None of us likes to be pushed into the place where we have to act differently, especially when we're not prepared. But then, the most traumatic moments often come when we least expect them.

We sometimes call this the locker-room mentality. Players and coaches go into the locker room before the game and again at halftime to work through their game plan. "This is what we're going to make happen."

And maybe it will happen that way.

The implication is that they decide what they will do before they get out on the field. They also know that they can plan, but they can't predict what will actually happen. When they're playing against another team, they may put their plan into effect and still end up defeated.

We can plan. We can hope. But we can't determine what will happen. And when those powerful events come and change our lives, some psychologists refer to them as *markers*. A marker can be something as simple as a girl wearing makeup for the first time or a teen getting his driver's license. Their lives are changed afterward, sometimes not dramatically, but life becomes different. We have markers all throughout our lives. They are those times that shout, "New chapter in life begins here!"

The man who lost his job, the woman who got shot in the face, the couple that lost their child to a drowning, the woman who lost her son in Iraq, the man whose wife left him, or the woman whose husband left her. Parents no longer speak to their children because of something they have done. Huge financial disasters befall a man and his life changes. All of these people experience markers.

I particularly want to focus on what we think of as the negative markers. If we persist and if we continue in our growth, at some point we are able to look back and see those same markers as positive. We can't rush the process, but the moment comes when we can even pause to give thanks to God for those events.

Regardless of what we call it, as soon as we realize we have a new marker, we have to reconfigure our lives. If we had an income of $100,000 last year and this year we must subsist on one-fourth of that amount, we must do a lot of difficult, painful rethinking of how we spend money.

We may have known what we wanted to do if life had continued as it was, but the rules have all changed. The markers force us to make a new game plan.

It's not easy to shift our way of thinking or move away from our old behavior, but that's what life's markers compel us to do. In the midst of that drastic shift, we should pause and ask, What does God want me to do?

As I point out elsewhere in this book, I had many lessons to learn after my accident. For example, I had to learn to accept help from others and how to take better care of myself. I could no longer rely only on myself. Could I have learned those lessons in other ways? Of course. But in the midst of my suffering I looked for God's hand at work and let him open my eyes and teach me compassion toward others. I don't think God caused that truck to plow into my car, but when I looked for some meaning in my tragedy it was as if I heard God say, "Follow this new path."

We can see a marker as one of the powerful moments in the life of Hagar, the servant wife of Abraham. She ran away because Sarah treated her badly. When she rested at a desert spring, God spoke to her and told her to go back. Not only did Hagar return but she also named the spot Beer-Iahairoi ("well of the Living One who sees me"). What she wanted to say to the generations after her was that God had always seen her, and now, in some form, she had "seen" the living God and it changed her life.

For some of us, like Hagar, it takes a serious marker in life for us to see God in our lives.

Dear God who sees all, thank you for seeing me. Sometimes I feel as if I'm totally alone and no one knows my plight—or cares. You care and I know you're with me. Don't let me forget. Amen.

You thrill me, Lord, with all you have done for me!
I sing for joy because of what you have done.
—Psalm 92:4[*]

44
CLOSE TO GOD

We've met too many people who never want to move beyond the past. They're locked into the way things once were. The character of Miss Havisham in *Great Expectations* by Charles Dickens is an excellent example. Her fiancé jilted her and her life never progressed beyond that day. Time stopped for her and she refused to move into the present. Her life revolved around getting married, and once her fiancé left her, nothing else had any value.

Even worse, she became a bitter woman, hated men, and taught her ward, Estelle, to detest men as well. As Dickens showed, Miss Havisham didn't just ruin her own life, but she influenced people and made life difficult for the hero, Pip, Estelle, and everyone else with whom she came into contact.

Miss Havisham is fictitious, but her character isn't. Many Miss Havishams live in our world.

When people struggle with change in their lives and get stuck, a good question I like to ask is this: When did you feel the closest to God? If they can remember and point to a time or place when they felt close, that's probably where they need to be again, but under new conditions.

When were those times? The moment we believed in Jesus Christ? When we were baptized? When we joined the church? Was it at a retreat? Some speak of feeling especially close to God when they read from the Bible. Some find their closest moments when they sing choruses or hymns and immerse themselves in music. We all have different ways in which we connect with God.

The task is to recover those special moments and ask ourselves about the conditions, our attitude, and our openness. When I can get people to answer the question and they reflect on a good time in their spiritual lives, they speak of it as a period when they felt peace or enjoyed their lives. They often remember joyful moments when, as one person said, "I felt I was ready to ascend to heaven." She knew that such an experience was possible again.

Once we've gone back to the time when we felt close to God, we can think positively about the present and move ahead to get closer to God once again.

The psalmist understood and began Psalm 92 with these

words, "It is good to give thanks to the Lord, to sing praises to the Most High" (Verse 1*). The entire psalm is a paean of praise and joy and wonder. That psalm writer connected with the living God.

So can we. If we remember the emotion of the past, we can recapture it in the present.

God, thank you for helping me think of the time when I felt close to you. Remind me of that time whenever I'm tempted to waver or get discouraged. I've been there before, I can tell myself, and I can become even closer because I've learned and grown through my experience. Thank you. Amen.

*. . . For I have learned to be content whatever the
circumstances . . . I have learned the secret of being content
in any and every situation, whether well fed or hungry,
whether living in plenty or in want.*

—Philippians 4:11b–12**

45

CONTENTED?

I constantly receive communications from people who have
bottomed out. They hurt; they want someone to listen.
They're desperate, and if they're desperate enough, they'll e-
mail a total stranger, pour their hearts out, and write gut-
wrenching stories. They're not sure where to turn or what to
do next. Sometimes, they're near the end and a few mention
taking their own lives.

Above, I used the term *bottomed out.* I understand that feeling. After my accident and during my 108 days in the hospital,
many, many times I was at that point of giving up. But God came
through for me, as he does for all of us if we open ourselves.
We're not beyond hope; we're not beyond God's loving touch.

For me, bottoming out has come to mean reaching the bottom of the pool where we can push off and zoom back toward the surface again. That's the message I try to give others. "If you're at the bottom of the pool, it's time to use that solid place to push off and get back to the top."

I told that to one man after he confessed that he didn't have any real friends and admitted that he avoided people at church who had reached out to him.

"Surround yourself with people who can help you," I urged him. I also challenged him to do at least one positive thing every day. That's the beginning of pushing off. That may sound like something small—and it is—but it's a beginning. When we're at the bottom of the pool, anything we do for ourselves is positive.

During my pain-wracked days in the hospital, I forced myself to look for something positive every day. The first few days demanded extreme effort but it got easier as I went along.

That's only the beginning. As we begin to view the positive factors in life, eventually we start to grasp the meaning of contentment. Paul provides a wonderful example to me. Some of his best writings came out of his times in prison. Dietrich Bonhoeffer is a more modern man who spent his last months in a German prison camp during World War II before he was executed. He left Germany when Hitler came to power, but he returned to his homeland in 1939, even though his friends urged him not to go back. He said he had to go back to show his solidarity with the suffering Christians in Germany. Like the apostle Paul, instead of feeling sorry for himself or complaining about the horrible conditions, he wrote to Christians and urged them to stand firm in their faith.

That's what contentment means: standing firm and saying, "I probably wouldn't have chosen to be here, but I'm at peace where I am." Part of contentment is to accept life as it is. It means to say (without anger), "This is the way life is. I accept my life as it is now and realize that God's loving arms are around me. With those loving arms around me, I can handle anything."

That's the concept of contentment—being at peace no matter what happens or how bad events seem. Paul wrote, "I have learned the secret of being content in any and every situation." It is a secret because so few are willing to accept what is right now and to be grateful. When I hit bottom in my pain, I was grateful I had enough energy to bounce back to the surface. And we can all do that. We can even learn to say, "This is where I need to be right now and I'm contented to be here."

God of all joy and peace, help me to live in a state of contentment. Remind me of your presence and your love that won't ever let me go. Even at the bottom of the pool, you're with me. If you're with me, I know I can make it. Thank you for giving me this hope. Amen.

For I am convinced that neither death nor life, neither
angels nor demons, neither the present nor the future,
nor any powers, neither height nor depth, nor anything else
in all creation, will be able to separate us from the love
of God that is in Christ Jesus our Lord.

—ROMANS 8:38–39***

46
THE SIZE OF OUR PROBLEMS

"Yes, I heard you speak, and I know you've got problems. So who hasn't?" the woman said to me at a signing. "No one is immune, and I think I've got as many as you have or maybe more."

She started to tell me her problems and she didn't hold back. Not only did she tell me an immense number of problems, but she spoke with great venom in her voice.

Finally I said, "You're extremely angry, aren't you? And you're miserable, too."

"If you had the hardships I've had to endure for the past thirty-seven years, you'd be miserable and complain, too."

I wanted to be kind, but she started on another litany of woes before I could interrupt her. When she paused, I said, "The misery of your life doesn't depend on the size of your problem."

She stared at me for several seconds before she said, "That's a stupid thing to say. Of course it does!" She went through a further recital of her problems, and they were serious.

At the end, I touched her hand and said, "I'm sorry." Those two words seemed to satisfy her. And I was sorry—sorry for her problems and sorry for her attitude.

What I tried to tell her is no secret. Any good therapist would have said the same thing: It's not a matter of the seriousness of the problem, but it's a matter of the seriousness of our attitude. It really comes down to how we accept our situation.

That incident reminds me of an e-mail someone sent me that contained a quote from Nietzsche that went, "He who has a *why* to live for can bear with almost *any how*." The woman who sent me the e-mail said that quote had caused her to examine herself. She was able to find something to live for and that had given her peace. The woman had an amazing story of being raped and beaten before her assailant slit her throat and left her for dead. A man out walking his dog discovered her body, used his cell phone to call 911, and saved her life. The ER doctor said that if the kind stranger had found her a few minutes later she would have bled to death. She is alive, but she had to go through fifteen surgeries.

"I'm not bitter," she wrote. "I was able to identify the man who grabbed me, and he's awaiting sentencing. Now I have to move on with my life."

She said that she lay in the ICU of the hospital for more than five weeks. Whenever she was conscious, she asked, "God, why did you spare my life?" She's a twenty-five-year-old teacher in an inner-city high school with a high immigrant population. She believes one reason she is still alive is so that she can work with those children and give them hope for a better life.

One day, when another teacher from the same school visited her in the hospital, she sat next to her bed and read the entire eighth chapter of Romans. "That's when I heard my answer," she said. "God had spared me for a purpose and I hadn't yet fulfilled my purpose."

In the final paragraph of her e-mail, she wrote, "Life ultimately means taking responsibility to find where I fit into this universe." She understood that truth even though her physical condition was worse than most of us would ever suffer. Even in the time of terrible suffering, nothing could take her away from God's love.

I wish all believers could understand this. It's not the size of the problems we face, but the attitude we have when we face them. The attitude makes the difference. If we can accept that God is truly with us, it doesn't matter what the trauma or disaster, we'll remind ourselves, nothing ". . . in all creation, will be able to separate us from the love of God. . . ."

God, forgive me for complaining about life being hard and unfair. Of course it's both. Instead, remind me that the tougher the problems, the greater your grace and the more I need you. Amen.

Always be full of joy in the Lord. I say it again—rejoice!
—Philippians 4:4*

47
Rejoice Always?

That's a rather strange command—to rejoice and to be full of joy. It's as if the apostle Paul commands Christians to be happy. And he does! Those words came out of Paul's experience so he knows it's possible. He tells his readers: Be filled with joy. Rejoice and keep on rejoicing.

Try to think of Paul when he wrote those words. He was in prison, and after years of teaching the gospel he was almost certain that the Romans would put him to death. He loved the people in the area around Philippi and expressed concern for them. Most of them were fairly new to the Christian faith. The words of the last chapter of his letter to them are his parting words. It's as if he says, "You probably won't ever see me again, because I'm going to die for the cause of Christ. Now here's what I want you to think and here's what I want you to do."

And the first thing for them was to rejoice. He could say that because he knew the *source* of joy—Jesus Christ. He wanted them to bubble over with joy, which is indicated by "I say it again—rejoice!"

Sometimes we receive joy by being in the presence of someone who cares about us, and their compassion and effervescence lifts us up. I have a few people in my life who always make me feel better about myself and about life just by being with them. They bring out the best in me and help me focus on the good, the positive, and the happy things.

This reminds Cec of a phone call he received one day from his best friend's coworker. "I can always tell when David has had lunch with you," he said. "When he returns to the office, he smiles more and his spirits are always lighter. You have that kind of effect on him."

That's a small picture to help us grasp what Paul meant. Our ultimate source of joy, however, is Jesus, and that's the secret Paul is trying to get across to the Philippians. The person he wants them to think about is the One Who Loves Them. That's the same message for us: Just being aware of God's presence is enough to raise our spirits. Joy comes when we pause to reflect on what God has already done for us and the hope of greater blessings that lie ahead. As we think of the victories and the blessings of the past, they not only give us the faith to look forward to new blessings, but they also enable us to rejoice.

Here's a helpful device so we can learn to rejoice constantly. When things look bleak or life seems unfair and against you, try this exercise. Sit down, relax, and close your eyes. Ask yourself, "What has God done for me? What blessings do I enjoy or take for granted?"

If we begin to focus our minds on what God has already done for us, we prepare ourselves to receive blessings today and in the days ahead. Joy increases joy. As we review what we have received in the past and as we open ourselves to receive, we make a life of joy possible.

One more thing: Rejoicing doesn't demand a particular form of behavior. It may show outwardly with smiles or calmness, but what really counts is the joy that comes from within, which carries itself to our face and even the way we move our bodies.

It is not only possible to rejoice at all times, but it's the way to live the victorious, overcoming Christian life!

God, I need your help. Too often I allow outward situations to determine my attitude and my joy or lack of it. Remind me now and each day that the source of my joy comes from an awareness of your presence with me to help me combat every obstacle. Amen.

Let everyone see that you are considerate in all you do.
Remember, the Lord is coming soon.

—PHILIPPIANS 4:5*

48

BECAUSE GOD IS NEAR

"You keep telling us you're not some holy saint," the woman said, "and I'm sure that's true. But you also tell me that you learned to love all people. You don't have enemies, so how can you be human?" She shook her head resolutely.

"Grams, it's okay," her teenaged grandson said.

"I try. I truly, truly try, but I just don't love everybody. Some people anger me and—"

"Wait a minute," I said, finally catching on. "You mean you don't *like* some people?"

"Of course that's what I mean."

"The Bible never says you have to like everyone; the Bible only commands you to love them."

"If there's a difference, I don't get it."

Our conversation went on for maybe twenty minutes and the one thing I had to keep saying to her is that she didn't understand the word *love* as used in the Bible. Almost everyone knows the noun form of Christian love is *agape*, but what they often don't get is that it's not an emotion, it's an act of the will. "It's an intention," I said.

I tried to explain to her that God doesn't ask or expect us to like everyone; he does expect us to love them. I read Philippians 4:5 to her in several versions. It's a verse difficult to translate because of the noun *epieikeia*. It's a word used in many ways, but most scholars believe it refers to forbearance and being patient with others.

"You mean just hanging in there with them when they do dumb things? Is that it?" her grandson said.

I smiled because I think she was catching on to the idea. I went on to point out that love means doing the best for others. It means wanting the best and doing the best to help others.

She finally understood, and she was able to realize that we do what we can to help others. She read the verse again: "Let everyone see that you are considerate in all you do." She smiled then. "If I truly love people, I'm considerate of their feelings, considerate of the way I treat them." She leaned closer and whispered, "Even if I don't like them or like their ways very much. Did I get that right?"

"Cool, Gram, cool!" yelled her grandson as he gave her the high-five gesture. He put his arm around her and started to walk away.

"There's one more thing to bear in mind," I said. "You have to pay attention to the rest of that verse."

She gave me a quizzical look and opened the Bible again and read: "Remember, the Lord is coming soon." I pointed out that if we believe we're only a heartbeat from heaven, our actions will show that. When we say the Lord is coming soon, it could be his second coming on earth or it may mean that we're ready to enter heaven. Either way, we need to be prepared.

"If I keep in mind that the Lord is not only near but is aware of the way I treat other people," she said, "then I'll act considerately and kindly. Is that what you mean?"

"Gram, it means you act just like Jesus is standing next to you every minute," the boy said. "If you think of the Lord walking beside you, how will you treat people?"

I wanted to hug that teen. He understood. Jesus is with us. When we go through difficult times, we do well to remind ourselves of that fact. But what about when we go through our day-to-day activities? What about the way we drive our cars? The way we treat people who are rude or demanding? I don't want to lay down a code of conduct for people, but that boy got it.

If we believe Jesus is right beside us all the time, it will show in the way we behave when coping with other people, especially those difficult, angry, and hard-to-get-along-with individuals.

> *Lord Jesus, you are beside me every moment. You see my actions. Help me to treat people right in everything I do. Remind me that I'm truly only a heartbeat from heaven. Because of that, I want to be caring and considerate of everyone I meet until the instant you call me home. Help me remember. Amen.*

Don't worry about anything,
instead pray about everything.

—PHILIPPIANS 4:6[*]

49
DON'T WORRY

Once I quoted Philippians 4:6 to a woman and she said, "What did Paul have to worry about? He didn't have a wife, a family, taxes, or a steady job. All he had to do was go from place to place and people fed him."

"So if you don't have any problems like the ones you mention," I said, "then your life is stress-free and worry-free?"

"I'm a good worrier, so I'd find something to worry about." She laughed.

I think she was right. Our human nature is always bent toward worrying and only by deliberate and decisive action can we change that.

The Philippians must have worried a lot or Paul wouldn't have made a point of urging them not to. As humans they were vulnerable to the changes and vicissitudes of life. For them, there was also the burden of being Christian in a world and in a time when their lives were in danger just for claiming faith in the Savior.

Paul couldn't deliver them, but he could plead with them not to worry. He explained to them that they really had no need to feel anxious. His words gently reminded them that God hadn't forgotten them. Someone once said, "Inner peace is the result of believing in prayer." He might also have said, "Inner peace is the result of believing in God's presence."

Paul's words echo those of Jesus in the Sermon on the Mount. He reminded his listeners that God provides for all of nature. "So I tell you, don't worry about everyday life— whether you have enough food, drink, and clothes. Doesn't life consist of more than food and clothing?" (Matthew 6:25*). After Jesus spoke of God's provisions for the birds and flowers he added, "And if God cares so wonderfully for flowers that are here today and gone tomorrow, won't he more surely care for you? You have so little faith!" (Verse 30*).

A friend once said that worry is negative faith. It's putting more trust in what will go wrong than it is putting trust in God's loving provisions. The message for each of us is quite simple: Don't worry.

If we worry, we have no peace. If we worry, we're filled with doubt. If we worry, we don't trust. So what's the solution? The only one Paul could offer them from hundreds of miles away was to pray. Ask God to help.

I remember seeing a film once in which four men were on a life raft during World War II as an enemy ship fired at them. One of them said, "Maybe we ought to pray."

"It's not bad enough yet," his friend said.

Which is where I see the big problem: We wait until things get bad, then we get desperate. Instead, Paul lays out a simple formula: Don't worry, but instead focus on God by focusing on prayer. It's that simple. It's not that easy to accomplish, but it does work.

When we remind ourselves that God is with us and already knows our dilemmas and problems, is there any cause to fret? And who would know the answer better than Paul the prisoner?

Dear God, I worry sometimes and doubt at others. I don't like that and I know it dishonors you. Help me to turn first to prayer. Help me to call on you for everything and then I won't have to resort to worry. Amen.

Tell God what you need,
and thank him for all he has done.
—Philippians 4:6b[*]

50

And Thank Him?

For 108 days, I lay in a hospital bed. My life as I had known it was shattered. I stared at my body—a physical mess—and I admitted to myself that I would never again be the healthy thirty-eight-year-old virile man I had once been.

My life had changed, and at first I tried to change it back. Somewhere during those weeks in the hospital and during the months of recuperation at home, I slowly accepted reality. Life wouldn't wait for me, and my physical body wouldn't change to fit my desires. I had to do something.

During that time, the fourth chapter of the book of Philippians began to take on new meaning. I have no idea how many times I had read the passage over the years, but I then read it differently. Paul wrote from prison to Christians who may have been undergoing persecution. This time I read it as a personal message from God to speed me on my way toward a new kind of life.

The first thing that amazed me was that instead of feeling sorry for himself, Paul exhorted—exhorted me—to move forward. As I personalized the message, he urged Don Piper to live faithfully and pleaded with me to stand firm "without being frightened in any way by those who oppose you" (Philippians 1:28*).

In Chapter 4, he guided me with practical advice. He presents a two-pronged approach. And I have learned that it does work for people like me. We must first figure out what we need and then we need to tell God. In that process, we thank God for all the things he's done in the past. And as we tell God what we need, we should take time to rethink our "needs." Too many of us get our wants and our needs confused. That was certainly true with me.

Paul went on to urge me to give thanks for the provisions of the past, and to give thanks in all things. That was difficult for me and I realize it must be difficult for many of us. When our lives aren't going as we like them to, how can we give thanks? How can we be thankful when our world has collapsed or turned upside down? How can we give thanks for the problems and the hardships and the pain?

As I continued to read those verses, I learned that instead of focusing only on my own pain and the terrible ordeal I was going through while I was in the hospital, I could move out of that self-defeating cycle. And I did! I was alive; my family and friends loved me. Members of our congregation did everything they knew to help. People from all over the country contacted me and said they were praying for me.

I must be honest: On some days I found it difficult to give thanks. Some days I could barely focus on anything positive, but as I improved, my thoughts became freer. I found things for which to be grateful—pain medication, nurses who treated me gently, friends who visited but didn't demand a lot of conversation, and cards and letters that encouraged me.

I did learn to tell God what I needed and to couple that with thanks. I'm convinced that all of us can do that. Part of preparing ourselves for the new normal is to assess where we are and accept the present. Part of accepting the present is to admit that life isn't hopeless and we don't have to live in despair.

Cec told me that years ago he went through a particularly dark period in his life. "I learned to thank God for the simple things in life," he said. "We expect our lives to be happy, trouble-free, and victorious. We forget that victories come only after we fight the things that try to hinder us."

That's part of giving thanks—to stop expecting life to be stress-free and without trouble, because problems are always there. Job had it nailed down when he said to his wife in the midst of all their troubles, "Shall we accept good from God, and not trouble?" (Job 2:10b**). But bigger than the problems are God's provisions.

*God, teach me to ask for what I need (and not just what I want).
As I do so, remind me of all your wonderful provisions in the
past. May your faithful provisions in the past encourage me to
believe in your faithfulness and to give even more thanks to
you. Amen.*

Don't worry about anything; instead,
pray about everything. Tell God what you need,
and thank him for all he has done. If you do this,
you will experience God's peace, which is far more
wonderful than the human mind can understand.
His peace will guard your hearts and minds
as you live in Christ Jesus.

—PHILIPPIANS 4:6–7*

51

GUARDING OUR PEACE

Even now, years later, I vividly remember the lack of peace I felt during the first of those months I had to stay in the hospital after my accident. Some days I worried that I wouldn't live; other days I worried that I wouldn't die, because I wanted to return to heaven. Even after I knew I wasn't going to die, many nights my mind wouldn't rest. I was in such pain I didn't know if I would ever stop hurting again. I could hardly think of anything except how bad I felt.

Physical pain is only one thing that destroys peace. I've

known other times when it wasn't physical pain that stopped me from enjoying serenity and calmness in God's loving presence. Rejection, dejection, fear, anxiety, worry—these are all manifestations of emotional pain that can cause turmoil in our souls.

When we set our minds toward something we want—and it's something we want very much—and we don't get what we yearn for, discouragement sets in. We fret and either try to discover reasons we didn't get what we want or we look inward and ask, "What's wrong with me?" When people treat us badly, we lose our inner tranquillity and our minds are agitated with feelings of revenge or hurt. When we feel unappreciated or unloved those feelings control our thoughts and we have no inner quietness.

At times like these we need God's peace to engulf us. Paul explains how to receive that peace: Don't worry, pray, tell God everything and be thankful. By following these guidelines we can rid our minds and hearts of troublesome, debilitating, and disheartening thoughts and experience greater closeness with God.

Too many people don't understand the meaning of Philippians 4:6–7. Paul instructed the Christians not to worry, but to pray. He urged them to tell God about *every need* and be thankful for what God has already done. If they did those things, the negative feelings would diminish and they would be open for God to fill their hearts with holy peace.

Paul didn't intend for those words to be a magic formula.

One must do more than just slavishly follow the four steps. These four things demand effort, introspection, and commitment, and they're not always easy. Sometimes we have to struggle to do what seems contrary to our human nature. But it is so worth the effort.

One woman told me, "You don't know what you're talking about. How can I be thankful when the whole world is pitted against me?"

"Look at what God did for you in the past," I said.

"That's the problem: It's all the past," she said.

I felt sorry for her because she couldn't move ahead and emerge as a tranquil person. She was stuck in her pain. The apostle told us what we need to do in order to achieve peace and this woman simply couldn't do it.

Paul didn't just give us a promise of peace. He used a Greek word (*phroureo*) that expressed military action. He wanted us to know that God functioned like a guard or an alert sentinel on duty.

The sentinel guarded and protected those inside the garrison. That's the same promise to us. I like to think of the Holy Spirit as a sentinel who is ready to defend us when any enemy tries to steal our inner peace.

Two millennia later it works if we follow God's divine instructions. It has certainly worked for me. I finally received peace during my convalescence. Many times since then I've sensed the Holy Spirit as my peace preserver.

Powerful Holy Spirit of God, remind me that you not only tell us not to worry, but you enable us to overcome our problems, and once we experience your peace, you are like an alert guard, ready to stop the invasion of worry and anxiety. Thank you, God. Thank you not only for your peace but also thank you for preserving my peace. Amen.

Finally, brothers and sisters, whatever is true,
whatever is noble, whatever is right, whatever is pure,
whatever is lovely, whatever is admirable—if anything is
excellent or praiseworthy—think about such things . . . -
And the God of peace will be with you.
—PHILIPPIANS 4:8–9[***]

52

FOCUS OUR THOUGHTS

"You can't stop your mind from thinking," one of my seminary professors said. "As long as you're conscious, your mind thinks. You can't stop the thoughts, but you can direct the flow."

During the long convalescence from my accident, I had plenty of time to think. I often had to force myself to focus on things actually worth thinking about. It was too easy to fall into self-pitying thoughts or to focus on what my life would have been like if only . . . if only I chose another route; if only the driver of the truck was more careful; if only things were different. Alone in my hospital room, my mind often drifted to thoughts of what might have been or thoughts of despair. I had to consciously force myself to think more productive thoughts: what I needed to do to heal; how I needed to adjust my life to the new normal; how I could use the gifts God had given me—both the gift of life and the glimpse of heaven—to benefit myself and others. He stressed the need for the right kind of thoughts. In another place, he wrote: ". . . We take captive every thought to make it obedient to Christ" (2 Corinthians 10:5**).

Perhaps he understood that if we think about something long enough, we tend to act on the results of our deliberations. If we learn to think along spiritual lines, we will also direct ourselves toward positive action. It's a law of nature that if we think about something often enough and long enough we reach the place where we can't stop thinking about it. The topic becomes obsessive. It's as if our minds start in a pattern and if we keep going over the same pattern long enough, the thinking becomes automatic. Our minds stay in a groove and we can't easily get them out of it.

If that's true, we need not only to put away negative thoughts, but we also need to get rid of what I call *unproductive* ones such as self-pity and self-shame. We need to contemplate peace, love, and happiness. Such thoughts make us content, able to enjoy our lives more.

In Philippians 4:8–9, Paul tells the believers to think about the things that are true, not to think negatively or deceptively.

If they think on things that are true, honest, and honorable, they will act with integrity and not have to be ashamed of what they do.

He goes on to urge them to focus on ideas that are noble or venerable. This is concerted, high-minded deliberation. This is the kind of thinking that keeps us from judging others' actions and motives and teaches us to be more accepting.

Philippians 4:4–8 contains a lengthy list of ways in which Christians need to train their minds to focus: think true, noble, right, pure, lovely, and admirable thoughts. I want to point out that the word *lovely* doesn't quite convey the apostle's original meaning. The Greek word could be translated as *those things that are lovable*. That is, we ought not to contemplate vengeance and punishment. Instead, if we set our thoughts on the lovely things such as kindness, sympathy, and acceptance, we do exactly what Paul commands. In all our thoughts, he wants us to ponder only the good. And we can learn to do that. It may not be easy, but we can discipline ourselves.

All these terms continue to remind us that as we think, so we are and so we act. "For as he thinketh in his heart, so *is* he," reads Proverbs 23:7 (†). We know that people who accomplish great things in life do so because they're single-minded. They are so wrapped up in what they consider important, they push away everything else.

As an example, once I had an appointment to interview a famous restaurateur. I went to the man's office and the room was filled with music—very, very loud music. The man wasn't even aware of the noise because he was totally concentrated on a report he was reading and had shut out every distraction. Until I sat down across from him, the man wasn't aware of my presence or anything except the report in his hands.

That's the kind of mind-set Paul urges: to have our minds so filled with the good things—the pure, lovely, and truthful—that there's no way for evil, harsh, mean, or unkind thoughts to get inside our heads.

God, teach me to keep my thoughts under control. Teach me to think about the things that build me up and encourage me. Remind me that my thoughts always come before my actions. Amen.

Finally, brethren, whatsoever things are true,
whatsoever things are honest, whatsoever things are just,
whatsoever things are pure, whatsoever things are
lovely, whatsoever things are of good report; if there be any
virtue, and if there be any praise, think on these things.

—PHILIPPIANS 4:8 †

53

THE JUPLER

The night before Thanksgiving (1957) my wife and I were in a head-on collision. The doctors didn't expect Shirley to survive the night and the staff allowed me to stay in the hospital room with her.

For three days, I (Cec) didn't know if she would live. The doctor and the nurses checked on her regularly. She breathed on her own, but she showed little response to treatment. "We'll have to wait and see" was always their answer.

I called relatives and friends for prayer, but I felt no peace. My emotions raced from high optimism to despair. One minute I surrendered her to God and two minutes later I begged

God to save her life. I prayed until I peacefully accepted whatever happened, then only minutes later would descend into a pit of bleakness and blackness.

Although I had my Bible, I couldn't focus on reading. That first night, perhaps an hour before daylight, I decided I had to read to find rest for my tormented soul. I opened my Bible, determined to study, but couldn't concentrate. I saw words but they meant nothing. I cried out for stillness in my heart, but nothing changed. I gave up, laid aside my Bible, and turned off the light in the small room.

After the room filled with darkness, I leaned back in the chair the nurse had brought for me and heard two words inside my head: *THE JUPLER.* That was enough, because I knew exactly what it meant. Although I liked to memorize Scripture, occasionally I'd have trouble remembering which phrase came first in a long passage. Shirley's mother used to come up with mnemonic devices for her own memorization. She gave me one to help me memorize Philippians 4:8 (in the King James Version) with only the consonants: TH JPLR. We added vowels and called it THE JUPLER. Those six consonants stood for true, honest, just, pure, lovely, and of good report. The verse ends by saying that "If there be any virtue, if there be any praise, think on those things."

I sat in the darkness and repeated the verse a seemingly endless number of times. Each time, my body relaxed a little. Peace slowly drifted into my heart. I still had no certainty that Shirley would survive, but I knew God would enable me to handle whatever happened. (She did survive and eventually walked out of the hospital.)

Christians not used to the King James Version don't always grasp the meaning of the way some terms are translated, but everyone can understand when Paul says to "think on these things."

I can offer no better suggestion when things go wrong than to ponder the positive, spiritual words from the Bible. Not only did they bring stillness to my soul, they have brought peace and assurance to millions over the ages, and they still work today.

Eugene Peterson freely translates these verses this way: "Summing it all up, friends, I'd say you'll do best by filling your minds and meditating on things true, noble, reputable, authentic, compelling, gracious—the best, not the worst; the beautiful, not the ugly; things to praise, not things to curse . . . Do that, and God, who makes everything work together, will work you into his most excellent harmonies" (Philippians 4:8–9 ††).

Wonderful, loving God, help me fill my mind with the best and the purest thoughts. Help me to keep my attention on you during the worst situations and you will give me your deep inner tranquility. You will take me through all the difficult times, and I'm grateful. Amen.

Do not be anxious about anything, but in everything,
by prayer and petition, with thanksgiving, present your
requests to God. And the peace of God, which transcends
all understanding, will guard your hearts and minds in
Christ Jesus.

—PHILIPPIANS 4:6–7**

54
IN EVERYTHING

"I pray a little now and then," a friend named Steve once said, "but my problems are so petty and God has much bigger, more serious things to take care of than to pay much attention to me."

"Where did you read that in the Bible?" I asked.

"Okay, I didn't read it, but—"

"But you've missed the point of prayer," I said. "Nothing is too small to bring to God. Besides, God doesn't have a limited number of lines open to hear petitions from us. He's able to hear and respond to every soul that cries out no matter when or how often."

"I guess I know that, but still—"

"No, I'm not sure you know—really know deep inside—or you'd think about God differently." I felt I had started to preach, but Steve was also serious, and I felt he needed help.

"I just don't want to trouble God."

I shook my head. Before I could answer, his son entered the room. I pointed to the four-year-old boy and said, "If he asks you for something, especially if it's something small, you'll ignore him, right?"

"No, I love doing things for him." Steve laughed.

He got the point. I wish everyone did. Nothing is too small for God's care and love, and there's certainly nothing too big. As our heavenly Father, God's act of love is to hear and respond to our cries. Our cries are not burdens or obligations. The all-powerful Creator and Savior wants to be the center of our lives and to be available no matter what our need. The Lord wants us to share every concern with him.

I thought of the words Paul wrote to his converts who were hundreds of miles away in distance and weeks away in travel time: "Do not be anxious about anything, but in everything, by prayer and petition, with thanksgiving, present your requests to God." Paul knew that prayer is a powerful cure for anxiety or worry. He stressed that we can take everything to God in prayer. *Everything*. That means we don't have to hold back anything.

Everything certainly includes praying for ourselves and our needs. I used to teach an adult Sunday school class. Years ago I asked members, "Is it all right to pray for our needs?"

Several people said, "That's selfish."

"Then why does the Bible tell us to pray for ourselves?" I asked. "Why do we pray for forgiveness? For guidance?" They sheepishly admitted that it was all right to pray for their own needs. "If those things are all right, is there a limit to what God wants to answer?"

I continued to stress that each person is valuable and loved. God delights to help us and wants to make our lives richer and better. Why is that selfish?

As I thought about that incident, I wondered if the answers were symptomatic of something else, something deeper. In Steve's case, was it really a matter of not bothering God? Or was it that Steve didn't feel worthy? Was it that he felt as if his life wasn't important enough? In short, despite what Steve said about his relationship to Jesus Christ, on some unconscious level, did he feel unloved?

As I've traveled around the country, I've sometimes become aware of such an attitude. The statements or questions vary, but deep inside, the issue is that some people don't feel good enough for God. I understand how that works. When we're emotionally beaten down and when life seems to pile more stuff on top of us, it's natural to feel as if we aren't deserving of

God's love and concern. We may put that into different words, but that's how we feel. If God really loves me, we think, I wouldn't have all this trouble.

I wish everyone knew and never doubted that God loves all of us, even in the midst of our trials and hardships. Our heavenly Father doesn't desert us when hard times strike. In fact, during those horrendous situations and in those tiny, everyday things, God's hand is stretched out and he whispers, "Don't be afraid. I'm here. I care."

Loving God, remind me, teach me, and help me to internalize this truth: You love me and nothing will ever diminish your love and compassion. Because you love me, you want to hear my every concern. You want me to cry out to you as you delight in answering. Remind me again—and again. Amen.

*Once you were dead, doomed forever because
of your many sins. You used to live just like the rest
of the world, full of sin, obeying Satan, the mighty prince
of the power of the air.*

—Ephesians 2:1–2*

55
Give Me a Mind Change

"I'm not who I used to be," my friend Barry said. "But I know who I'm becoming even though God isn't finished with me." He told me how much comfort he had found when he compared Barry BC (before Christ) with the Barry of today. "That helps me when I get down on myself, especially when I hear myself saying, 'By now I ought to have . . .'"

That was a wonderful insight for me. When we look at where we were and compare it with where we are now, how can we not be encouraged? I think that's what Paul meant at the beginning of the second chapter of Ephesians. He described those outside of Christ: They were spiritually dead. He said to the Christians, "That's who you used to be. You were once spiritually dead, but now you're alive." They knew they were alive because they had taken control of their lives away from Satan and had given it to Jesus Christ.

Many Christians don't think like those who are spiritually alive. They haven't learned that they have new minds and they can focus on a higher plane and live with superior values. Paul put it this way: ". . . Let God transform you into a new person by changing the way you think. Then you will know what God wants you to do, and you will know how good and pleasing and perfect his will really is" (Romans 12:2*).

Barry told me that he had heard for years about the need to control his thoughts and not be overcome by lustful and negative thinking. He just didn't think it was possible, or at least not possible for him. One day he saw a sign, which was a cartoon of a car with big eyes for front headlights and tears flowed from them. Underneath were the words, "I'm suffering. I need an oil change."

As he read those words, Barry thought, "I need a mind change." He pulled his car to the side of the road and prayed, "God, you gave me a new birth in Christ, now I need to change—to be able to think and behave like your child. You adopted me into your family and I need a mind change."

He prayed for several minutes before peace came to him. From then on, he made a constant effort to refocus his thoughts. He began in small ways. One of the first things was his grudge against his former wife, Marian, who refused to let him see the children regularly. He wrote the following prayer on a card and kept it in his shirt pocket: "God, help me to think kind and generous thoughts about Marian." He said he had to pray that way every day, many times every day, but he finally was able to overcome his pent-up anger.

"I truly received a mind change," he said. "That's the only way I know how to express it."

From there, Barry tackled other issues in his life by praying almost the same prayer. He hated his job and he prayed, "God, help me to think kind and generous thoughts about my responsibilities here and about the people with whom I work." Slowly his attitude changed.

This wasn't easy—radical changes never are—but it was possible. Barry's story resonates with me because I struggled—and still do—over the same things. I've had to push away the disappointments and hurts. I've been to heaven and back, but that didn't make me perfect. It did give me a greater desire to live so that everything I do pleases God.

I haven't won total victory, but I know we can overcome the mind-set that chains us to old thought patterns of anger, self-pity, and indifference. God is in the mind-changing business.

Dear mind-changing God. I thank you for the changes you've made in my life. Help me to want to continue to change, and please continue to show me how to change. Amen.

Therefore, in order to keep me from becoming conceited,
I was given a thorn in my flesh, a messenger of Satan,
to torment me.

—2 Corinthians 12:7***

56
When Life Gets Hard

"The Bible is filled with the chronicles of people's difficulties," I said the other day. I hadn't thought about that before. The Bible portrays problems, disasters, and disappointments in the lives of people. As we read, we learn they either overcame or succumbed. Many people see their lives the same way with not much else in between. It's black or white; they succeed or they fail; they win or they lose. It's all or nothing. Maybe that's why they seem to lead despondent, despairing lives. If their life isn't absolutely perfect, if everything doesn't go their way, then their life is a complete failure. And we know no one's life is perfect.

So imperfect people with imperfect lives (and that is all of us) bemoan the fact that things aren't completely perfect instead of being happy and enjoying what is good. They read in the Bible about contentment, peace, and victory and wonder how they missed out. In their worst moments, they examine their lives and have trouble focusing on anything positive.

I have three things to suggest (learned from personal experience) when life gets really hard. First, we need to make the assumption that there is a divine purpose behind the difficulties. Nothing happens by accident. Nothing happens to us outside of God's notice. If we're Christians, that's an assumption we can have because we serve a loving, all-powerful God.

Look to the apostle Paul for guidance. Besides the physical pain, he was shunned, rejected, and despised. One of the things that made that man so remarkable was that he believed God had a purpose in everything that happened to him. Granted that none of us are like Paul and our lives aren't in constant danger. We don't face the horrible persecutions he endured. His life was far more extreme, and perhaps that's why he understood something significant and could stand firm: He knew God had a purpose.

Paul understood much and had an amazing number of divine revelations, but God didn't want him to become puffed up with pride. God gave him what Paul referred to as a "thorn in my flesh, a messenger of Satan." We don't know what either term means, but we do know God had a reason for sending the thorn. It wasn't a capricious act; it was to keep him humble.

Paul begged for deliverance and the Lord answered, "My

grace is sufficient for you . . ." (2 Corinthians 12:9***). Again, that's the point: God had a purpose and he remained with Paul in the midst of his suffering.

Second, God might reveal the purpose for our difficulties, however, God might not reveal them. In those moments, we need to think of God's words to Israel: "The secret things belong to the LORD our God, but the things revealed belong to us and to our children forever, that we may follow all the words of this law" (Deuteronomy 29:29***).

In effect, Moses said to the people, God has secrets—hidden things—that we may never understand in this life. God doesn't choose to make everything known to us, but God does reveal enough for us to obey.

I don't know why we have so many problems and hardships. It's not my divine calling to explain God's purposes or patterns. What I can do is affirm that God has a reason, yes, a divine purpose, behind everything that happens in our lives.

Where does that leave us? It leaves us with a choice. If we can honestly say God has a purpose in the terrible things that happen to us, our major responsibility is to figure out how we can best serve that purpose. It doesn't mean we have to figure out the reason behind it. God calls for our loving obedience to the tasks we have. Just that.

It's often not an immediate revelation or any high-level calling. I believe my purpose at this stage of my life is to spread my story of life after death and life and a meaningful life before death. I didn't grasp that fact in 1989 or 1990 or even in 2000. Now I get it because I'm doing what I believe God has called me to do.

The psalmist cries out, "I desire to do your will, O my God" (Psalm 40:8**). That's also my prayer, and I frequently pray that I'll always delight in obeying God's will.

The third thing to help when life gets hard is to remember that God's grace is always sufficient for every problem and for every moment we're alive. The Bible assures us that God won't put a load on us heavier than we can handle. I know that, but during my recovery there were times when I was in such pain that I thought it was more than I could handle.

Somehow I did handle it. I learned I had a stronger desire for survival than I would have believed. I learned many things about myself and I also grew spiritually in those horrible moments. I hope never to have that kind of pain again, but I know that God was by my side every second and his grace was as sufficient then as it is in any need we have.

God, I don't see a lot of purpose in the problems I face. I wonder why such things happen to me. Help me to get my attention off the reason and to concentrate on obeying what I already know to do. Help me to do what you've already shown me to do with my life. Amen.

[Jesus said,] He gave five bags of gold to one, two bags of gold to another, and one bag of gold to the last—dividing it in proportion to their abilities—and then left on his trip."

—MATTHEW 25:15*

57

THE HAPPIEST PEOPLE

I like to be around happy people—genuinely happy people—those individuals who radiate an inner joy that shows on their faces. It's obvious they truly enjoy being alive. Happy people like the work they do, the families they have, and the churches they attend.

Material acquisitions and a long list of achievements aren't prerequisites for happiness. Achievement doesn't have a lot to do with happiness. If it does, then I wonder why I've met so many successful-but-miserable people. However, I have met people without college degrees, fancy titles, or a corner office who just bubble with joy. The other day I was at a local retail shop and as I waited for my credit card charge to go though, I noticed how happy the cashier was. The woman greeted everyone and seemed to know many of them by name. Behind her was a plaque that honored her for twenty-five years of service.

"You've been here a quarter of a century," I said. "That's a long time in one job."

"Oh, this is the perfect job for me," she said. "I love what I'm doing and everyone is friendly and wonderful."

As I tucked away my credit card receipt, I thought, they're friendly because you give them a smile and a warm welcome. You spread your happy virus.

Yes, I also meet grumpy people, and I find them in every walk of life. But the best days are when I meet those effervescent individuals whose presence changes the atmosphere around them. Unconsciously, they uplift the spirits of everyone around them. When I meet happy people, they're often unaware of their effect on others. They simply enjoy their lives and see their work as service.

For example, five of us arrived at O'Hare in Chicago quite early for our flight. The Delta gate agent said, "It's raining over most of the Southeast and Southwest. Why don't I book you on the flight that leaves in about half an hour? Because of the storm, there won't be any extra charge."

I didn't have to ask if he liked his job. His face radiated a pleasure in serving us. When we thanked him for being so thoughtful, he said, "I'm glad when I can do little things like this to help others." (Our plane encountered only a little rain on the trip. After we landed in Houston, we learned that our scheduled flight had been cancelled because of severe thundershowers.)

When I see people who love their work, such as the cashier or the gate agent, they radiate an infectious joy. I love to watch them at work. They give of themselves and people respond. They're not only happy, but they make the world a happier place. I understand that attitude.

When I was a DJ as a young man out of college, I would almost have paid the station to let me play music. I did what I loved, and the money was truly secondary.

I often think that Christians should stand at the front of the line. Of course, that isn't always the way it works; there are many Christians who are unhappy. But I have to ask myself why. I know we have the spiritual resources. We have the Holy Spirit and the Holy Book. We know Jesus. We know that God put us here for a divine purpose. That should fill us up with unrestrained joy.

But that's not always the case. I think the problem is that many of us have to discover the will of God to enjoy our lives. Years ago the Billy Graham Evangelistic Association put out a tract with the title, "How to Have a Full and Meaningful Life." I've forgotten the details of the tract but I can't forget the title. Isn't a full and meaningful life what we all yearn to live? I didn't say happy, delirious, or thrilling. We have those feelings, but what I want to stress is a full and meaningful life.

If we lead the full and meaningful life, we're doing God's will, the Lord is glorified, and life is good.

As I think about the will of God, I'm reminded of a story Jesus told, often called the parable of the talents. (A talent was a large sum of gold that weighed about seventy-five pounds.) A man went on a trip and gave three servants money to invest while he was gone. "Dividing it in proportion to their abilities" is the clue to the purpose of the story.

The man with five bags of gold doubled his investment and so did the one with only two. The third one, who was less able and received only a single bag of gold, did nothing with it. He's also the one with whom the boss became angry when he returned.

The first two were the happy people. They did what they could with the ability they had. They're the ones to whom the man said, "Well done, my good and faithful servant" (Verses 21 and 23). The third, a fearful man, did nothing with what he had been given, even though he had only a small amount and his boss expected few results. When the servant did nothing, however, he heard these words, "You wicked and lazy servant!" (Verse 26).

Do you want to be happy? It's not that difficult. We do what we can with the ability we have. It's that simple. As the story teaches, God doesn't ask us to be what we're not. He wants us to work in proportion to our abilities. If we give what we have, that's all God asks. If we give of ourselves to others, not only are we happy in what we do, but we also spread joy to others.

God, sometimes I think I'd like to do big, wonderful things for you. Help me to realize that big results aren't what you ask. You ask me to faithfully use the abilities and the opportunities you've given me. If I use them, I know I'll have a full and meaningful life. That is, I know I'll be happy. Thank you, God. Amen.

*"Keep this Book of the Law always on your lips;
meditate on it day and night, so that you may
be careful to do everything written in it.
Then you will be prosperous and successful."*

—JOSHUA 1:8***

58

DO I WANT TO KNOW
GOD'S WILL?

Perhaps that sounds like a strange question, because we constantly speak about the topic. *But do we want to know—really?*

The more I travel, the more I suspect the answer is, "Uh, well . . ."

One reason some people don't know (or want to know) the will of God is because they're afraid they might not like what they hear.

It reminds me of a woman I know who had gone to the doctor for tests for cervical cancer. She never called the doctor to get the results. When I asked why, she said, "I don't want to know." She was afraid of what she would hear. Her fear wasn't going to change anything, but she decided she'd rather live without knowing than to face the possible negative results. (She did have cancer. She survived, but only because the doctor contacted her.)

With some Christians, it seems as if they dread to know. Maybe they're afraid that God really doesn't like them and wants them to do something they won't like. They may be afraid that God will demand more from them than they're prepared to give. In their fear or hesitancy, they miss one important element: *God wants the best for us.*

God wants to bless us, to enrich our lives, and to make us happier, more fulfilled individuals. Sometimes that may be difficult to grasp, especially when we're skidding downhill fast.

Maybe we don't want to know God's will because we don't think we deserve the good things. Maybe we don't want to know because that knowledge may demand a greater commitment than we've made so far.

Maybe we're afraid that God will ask us to do exactly what we don't want to do. I've heard people give testimonies like that—and I sometimes question such statements. God doesn't want unwilling, angry, and belligerent followers. If we truly believe God loves and wants only the best for us, it doesn't make sense that God would then say, "Okay, the worst thing you can think of is to become a missionary in India. That's exactly what I want you to do—just because you don't want to go."

Does that sound like God?

One thing that helps me grasp that reality is the use of familial terms in the Bible. God our *Father*, says a great deal about the relationship. We're also called children of God and sometimes sons and daughters of God. The Jews lived in rural settings and they readily understood when the psalmist called them the sheep of his pasture. Jesus also refers to himself as the Good Shepherd (see John 10).

One reason for such familiar terms is that it enables us to see how God works in our lives. Our heavenly Father wants us to do the things that are best for us and at the same time glorify him. That's why we were made: to be wholly and completely fulfilled in his service.

As in God's instructions to Joshua, if we focus on God's words and obey what we read, God blesses our way. That sounds like a wonderful way to live, doesn't it?

God, teach me your will. Keep me open so that I can hear anything and everything I need to do your will. Remind me that you only want the best possible life for me. Amen.

[Jesus] . . . knelt down and prayed, "Father,
if you are willing, take this cup from me; yet not my will,
but yours be done."
—LUKE 22:41–42[**]

59

I DON'T WANT TO SUFFER

I heard a lecture when I was a student in seminary that greatly impressed me. The speaker (whose name I don't remember) said that the meaning of life changes, but it doesn't cease to be. That was such an odd statement, which is probably why I remember it. He meant that we never fully grasp the meaning of our life. About the time we have it all figured out and say, "Oh, now I can see where my life is going," changes throw us into a sharp curve and the way is again obscured.

He also pointed out that those who live in disappointment and despair are often those who want to hold on to a meaning or state of being and aren't open to anything new. I've often referred to them as the people who groan, "I want my life to be the way it used to be." And it never will be the same again, especially after they've gone through severe trauma.

The speaker listed several ways we could find meaning in life. He made it clear that Jesus Christ is the center of life and we can't truly find answers until we make him our starting point.

He went on to say that we discover meaning in three different ways. First, by the work we do or the lifestyle we lead. We follow the path that's most natural for us whether it's to be as a hermit, a sales executive, or a lawyer. If we do the work for which God has suited us, we find meaning. We are also able to say, "This is what I was meant to do."

For example, Cec was a teacher, a missionary, and a pastor before he became a full-time writer twenty years ago. When he speaks about his life, he'll tell you how much he enjoyed everything he did, but as a writer, all those experiences came to fruition. "This is what I was meant to do," he has said many times. I could say the same thing about being a preacher and a public speaker. It's as if everything in my life has slowly come together to make me ready for what I do now.

A second way to find meaning is when we experience those special individuals who enrich our lives. Their influence brings meaning. They can be spouses, friends, or teachers. These are the people who love us unconditionally, who accept us as we are. Because we feel their loving acceptance, they enable us to enjoy ourselves more and, in the process, life takes on more meaning. Their influences enable us to experience truth, love, or goodness.

The third thing the speaker said was that we find meaning by our attitude toward unavoidable suffering. Several times he pounded out the phrase *unavoidable suffering*.

He wanted to make the point that we find meaning in life even when we're confronted with seemingly hopeless situations. Those things can't be changed and they are the times when the worst possible problems bombard us. That's also the time when we learn who we truly are. We can turn our personal tragedies into triumphs or we can wallow in our hardships.

A few years ago I read a remarkable book called *Tuesdays with Morrie*. A professor from Brandeis University, Morrie Schwartz, was dying with ALS—Lou Gehrig's disease. The thin volume contains lessons about how to live while we're in the process of dying. Mitch Albom (the writer) found meaning in life through that encounter. I also wonder if Morrie himself found meaning because he was able to pass on his wisdom and understanding to one of his favorite pupils, and he grew in the process of passing on what he experienced.

Morrie suffered, but he didn't suffer as if life had no meaning and no value. His last days gave hope and encouragement to others to live.

God, we all search for meaning, and I certainly do. I yearn to find meaning in the things I do and among the people I meet, but I don't like to suffer. I wish there were easier ways to learn. Help me to see that the easy way may not always be your way. Amen.

How long, Lord? Will you forget me forever?
How long will you hide your face from me?

—PSALM 13:1[***]

60

GOD'S HIDDEN FACE

Cec went through an intense period of darkness for about eighteen months. Here is how he tells it:

One day I realized that I had no sense of God's presence. I felt empty, alone, as if God had vacated my life. My faith didn't evaporate and I didn't doubt the existence of God, yet for reasons I couldn't understand, God simply stopped communicating with me.

I examined my heart countless times. I confessed and reconfessed every known trespass and failure and prayed for God to forgive me the sins of ignorance, but nothing changed. The best way I could explain it was to think about walking outside on a night when the clouds totally cover the horizon. They hide the stars and the moon, even though I know they're there. That's how I felt about God.

I continued to pray daily and I read my Bible even more zealously. (I read it, but the words seemed lifeless and empty.) One day, I read Psalm 13 where the psalmist cried out about God hiding his face. I kept searching and discovered more than a dozen references in the Old Testament to God's hidden face. One of them that stood out was Psalm 30:7***: "O Lord, when you favored me, you made my royal mountain stand firm; but when you hid your face, I was dismayed."

For those in ancient times, God's face referred to the presence of God. The expression "to see the face of God" meant to appear in the sanctuary or to have communion with God, or to receive divine help when needed, or to be blessed and protected. When there was no awareness of God's presence they referred to God's hidden face.

God's hidden face? I asked. Isn't God always reaching out and making himself known? Why would God hide or be hidden from believers? And yet in the Psalms David said more than once that God had done just that.

As I thought and prayed each day, I realized that David would surely have understood what it was like to be an outcast from the people of Israel. As he fled from Saul for years, surely he must have felt God had hidden his face.

In my own life, day followed day and nothing changed. My friends seemed blessed and excited by God's presence. I still went to church; I still taught my Sunday school class. Nothing changed outwardly for me, except that I couldn't understand why God had chosen to cut off communication with me.

That went on for eighteen months and God never showed me a reason, but I did learn several valuable lessons about myself. I also sensed that one day the darkness would dissipate and God would smile on me once again.

Eventually, the light began to shine again—not bright, but at least it was light. Over the next few months, I sensed God smiling on my life once again.

As I look back, I realize that all of us have dark periods and for some they last longer than for others. Don's came from 108 days in the hospital and thirty-four surgeries. My darkness was internal. I can say clearly in retrospect that the methods God uses aren't as important as the results. If we focus on the light ahead and not on the present darkness, we may not understand why things happen, but we do know that even the worst of times are temporary times.

My period of darkness made me stronger, more committed to Jesus, and more focused on my faith. Like Don, I've also realized that there are blessings from going through the dark places, especially because we didn't choose the darkness. The best we can do is obey while we travel onward through the darkness.

God of light, I don't like darkness and I want to feel your smile on me all the time. Help me so that when those dark moments come, I'll know you haven't forsaken me or stopped loving me. Fill me with hope and the realization that, like David, I'll see your face once again. Amen.

Do not repay anyone evil for evil. Be careful to do what
is right in the eyes of everyone. If it is possible, as far
as it depends on you, live at peace with everyone.
Do not take revenge, my dear friends . . . for it is written:
"It is mine to avenge; I will repay," says the Lord.

—ROMANS 12:17–19***

61

GETTING EVEN

"You mean you never thought, not even once, of going to the driver and bashing in his face?"

The man's question shocked me and I shook my head. I had told him that I never met the driver, who was an inmate in a nearby prison. By the time I was well enough to visit him, he had been released and gone to San Antonio.

"But look what he did to you!"

I understand the anger of the man who asked the question. He wasn't really upset because I hadn't retaliated; he was upset over his own situation. He had received a double blow in his life. He had lost his job on Friday and on Saturday his wife had left him, even though he said there was no connection between the two events.

He tried to project his anger onto me. Part of that anger, I felt, was that he couldn't find anyone to blame. His company was losing money and they fired their last-hired employees. He and his wife had argued and screamed at each other for months, although he claims they sincerely loved each other. He wanted to retaliate—to get even for what had happened to him.

He kept saying, "But he killed you. He ought to have been executed or at least to have spent the rest of his life behind bars."

"What would you have done?" I finally asked.

His mouth twisted and he threw out all kinds of things he would have done to the driver. I felt sorry for him because he could think only of right and wrong and nothing in between. He was determined to see only punishment and vengeance. To him, the driver had been guilty, and because he had done such a terrible thing, he should have been punished. There were no extenuating circumstances.

"But if you beat up the driver [one of his responses]," I asked, "would that be right? Wouldn't it be wrong for you to hurt him?"

I don't think I changed the man's mind, because retaliation seems like a natural response to him, as it does to many. "Someone hurt me so he has to pay for it." But none of us, according to the New Testament, has the right to do wrong, not even if the first wrong has been done to us.

What I also thought about was the way retaliation escalates. Suppose I had visited the driver and beaten him. Okay, I would have had to get someone else to do it for me. What next? Quite likely, he would feel he had to retaliate against me, but not just get even. He would increase my punishment. Maybe he'd break both my legs. And then, of course, I couldn't let him get away with that. If played out, one of us would have murdered the other.

I've also seen this matter of getting even take place with words between husbands and wives, parents and children, and among once-close friends. Once the battle starts, it's natural to retaliate with a bigger gun or a more powerful argument. The only way to end the dispute is for someone to raise hands in surrender.

But here's a better idea: *Don't start.*

If we're wronged, isn't that God's business to settle? Isn't God the Just One, the one who settles all things and makes them right? It may not happen now, but one day, and that may be Judgment Day, we'll all have to give account.

Isaiah prophesied about Jesus and said, "He was oppressed and afflicted, yet he did not open his mouth; he was led like a lamb to the slaughter, and as a sheep before its shearers is silent, so he did not open his mouth" (Isaiah 53:7***). That's our example. It's also given to us in the words of Paul, who writes, "Let no debt remain outstanding, except the continuing debt to love one another, for whoever loves others has fulfilled the law" (Romans 13:8***).

There is one way to retaliate: We give back with love. We become the epitome of kindness and caring. My agent, Deidre Knight, said that through prayer and through doing kind deeds, she "love bombs" those who hurt her.

Isn't that an excellent way to get even?

God of justice and God of love, sometimes it's hard not to scream out because life seems unfair and people don't always do the right thing. I want to fight back, but help me realize that I have only one responsibility: I am responsible to care about them. Help me, please help me do that. Amen.

Bless those who persecute you; bless and do not curse.
Rejoice with those who rejoice;
mourn with those who mourn.

—ROMANS 12:14–15[**]

62

COMPASSION

While I lay in bed for 108 days without being able to get up, I learned a great deal about myself, and some of it I hadn't wanted to know. I saw the worst side of myself. Of course, I'm sure they were things others had observed. The best part is that even when I was at my worst, my family still loved me, my friends stayed with me, and the church didn't desert me.

In reflection (and it can only come after the event), I now look back at my own difficulties and remember. Because I remember, I can translate those painful days into an understanding of the pain and difficulties others go through. Because I've felt extreme physical pain—and still do—it's easy for me to empathize with other people who are physically hurting.

Maybe members of groups such as Alcoholics Anonymous are right when they sometimes say to nonalcoholics, "You don't know what it's like to be addicted to alcohol." I don't argue. They are so taken up with their own problem of recovery, of crawling out of their deep hole, and of moving beyond wanting another drink, they can see little else. At that stage, they're correct: I can't understand.

But once they move beyond the early stages, once they live on a level beyond mere abstinence, they begin to realize they are not quite so unique after all.

It doesn't matter whether the subject is addiction, temptation, pain, or blessing, none of us is truly unique. We may feel that we are. In the early days, which may be the days of recovery or the time we seek the new normal for our lives, we usually feel as if no one else has ever walked down the same path. We can't hear other people because we're too focused on ourselves—on our traumas and the changes going on in our lives.

I don't want to rob anyone of that experience. We *need* to have a time when we feel unique, different, and separate from the rest of the world. During that transition time, we often express the most negative thoughts and assume no one else in the entire universe has ever felt exactly the same way. It's not a logical response; it's an emotional reaction. We really don't care if others have felt the same way. It's as if to say, "This is my exclusive time when I feel totally different from anyone else. No one can possibly understand."

Once we've started to move forward, we recognize that we did go through a transition stage. Once we recognize whatever we need to be after licking our wounds, feeling sorry for ourselves, and isolating ourselves from others, we're ready to move back into the real world again.

But we don't reenter the way we went out. Things have changed. Our attitudes are different; we perceive people and events in new ways. We may not be aware of the changes, and sometimes the new attitudes may be subtle.

Two positive things strike me about moving out of the period of isolation. First, we're softer, we're kinder, less demanding, and not as judgmental. (Of course, we can become bitter, angry, and filled with hatred, and I have witnessed that many times. As the saying goes, some became bitter, others became better.)

Second, we come out wiser. We used to know all the answers but no longer. Now we're satisfied with not knowing the solution to every problem. As we reemerge, we feel less confident and we boast less. If we've learned, we're slower to criticize, reluctant to point fingers at others, and more tolerant of people who disagree with us.

When Paul wrote Romans 12, he wrote as an older Christian and as a man who had experienced rejection, persecution, and hardship. Instead of being bitter, his words overflowed with compassion. He told them to bless those who persecuted them—to do whatever good for them they could. They were to rejoice in others' successes and mourn for others' pains. Paul could write that because he had been transformed. And that's what God wants for each of us. He wants us to be different but different in a more compassionate way.

God of compassion, help me accept others more readily. Help me to think kindly and speak generously of others. Because I've experienced grace, compassion, and understanding, please help me to pass it on. Amen.

. . . The Lord appeared to Solomon during the night in a
dream, and God said, "Ask for whatever you want me to
give you." . . . "Now, O Lord my God, you have made
your servant king in place of my father David . . .
So give your servant a discerning heart to govern
your people and to distinguish between right and
wrong . . ." . . . The Lord was pleased that
Solomon had asked for this.

—1 Kings 3:5–10 **

63

GOD HAS GOTTEN BIGGER

Try to imagine the scene when Dick Onarecker got inside my wrecked car, placed his right hand on my right shoulder, and passionately prayed for me. He did this despite the fact that both EMTs had told him I was dead. Dick was a Baptist preacher. Baptist preachers don't believe in praying for dead people. It's not part of their theology. I'm a Baptist preacher, too, so I know.

But right then, theology didn't matter. God wanted obedience. He wanted Dick to do what he told him to do, so the pastor put theology aside (not a bad thing to do sometimes) so he could focus on God's will, which was to pray for a dead man in a wrecked car. Had Dick consulted his theological framework, he probably would have refused to obey, but instead he chose to listen to the Holy Spirit that prompted him. He prayed and God answered his prayer: I returned to earth.

Since those days I've thought about my theology. The word *theology* really means a study of God, but in practical terms, it refers to what we believe about God. I'm a seminary graduate, I've read the orthodox books, and I've heard the best sermons, but in one way my theology has changed after the accident: God became bigger than he was back then.

Okay, that's my perception of course. God isn't more powerful in reality, but he is in my understanding. My concept of God was too small and too limited. My encounter with him is so much more powerful than it was before that morning in January of 1989. Call it practical theology, if you like, but I know I perceive God differently today than I did before.

My theology changed because I had to learn to lean on him, which wasn't part of my lifestyle, despite my words and despite my desire to do so. I had to depend completely on God for everything. And I truly mean everything. The truth is we've always been dependent but we don't acknowledge or want to recognize it. I had what some have called a rude awakening to reality.

Too often we fail to grasp that God is the provider for everything. My theological training taught me that, but my accident enabled me to experience it. For me, the single most important thing that came out of the accident is that I can admit (and rejoice) that I truly am dependent on my relationship with God for everything: everything from my ability to get out of bed in the morning to the strength to complete my tasks for the day, and for guidance and wisdom. For example, I ask for wisdom a lot more now than I used to. I used to ask for strength, now I ask mostly for wisdom.

I believe a prayer for wisdom honors God. When that's what Solomon requested, God was pleased. The new king didn't ask for wealth or the death of his enemies, and God said, "Since you have asked for . . . discernment in administering justice . . . I will do what you have asked. I will give you a wise and discerning heart . . ." (1 Kings 3:11–12 **).

I didn't get a heaping amount of wisdom the way Solomon did, but I am wiser today. Yes, God has gotten bigger in my life. That stack of sermons beside me in the car on the day of the accident was a testimony to what I preached; now my life is a testimony to what I practice. That accident started the change in my life. It was a powerful turning point and God has become so much bigger!

Great God, become bigger in my life. I believe in you now, but I want more. I want to be more open, more understanding, and wiser. Thank you that you can provide all of that, and you can also grow bigger in my life. Thank you. Amen.

Now to him who is able to do immeasurably more than all we ask or imagine, according to his power that is at work within us, to him be glory in the church and in Christ Jesus throughout all generations, for ever and ever! Amen.

—Ephesians 3:20–21[**]

64

BETTER THAN THE BAD

Even before my accident I used to pray for people who were hurting. They had truly sad stories: "My wife left me." "I lost my job." "I was sexually molested." "Both of my kids are on drugs." I had one special prayer. After I talked to God about their needs, I concluded with these words, "I pray that you will make what will happen as good as this experience has been bad."

I meant these simple words before my accident, and since my accident, I mean them even more. I only have to look at my own life and know that God has answered my prayer. I don't have a perfect life, and I battle physical pain every single day, but my life is as good now as it was bad after my accident in 1989. In fact, it's better now.

I can testify that over a period of years, many times my prayers were answered. I mean graphically and powerfully answered, in a way that exceeded even what I could have imagined.

It was as if I had sat there in the face of the serious problems that confronted these people and asked, "What would be the best possible thing that could happen?" And I did ask that question often. We let our imaginations run wild, and their situations ended up better than we could ever have guessed or asked.

And why not? God's in the better-life-ahead business. That's what God does for us. That's why God is the founder and owner of Hope Universal and Life Eternal—it is one of the thousands of ways he showers his love on us.

Again, I look at my new normal, that is, my life since 1989. In some ways what's happened is far, far better than I could have ever imagined. It doesn't mean that my situation wasn't bad, because it was bad. Even now, I have constant reminders of my limited physical capacity. But God gave me more strength, joy, and a positive attitude than I had ever imagined possible.

I was a pastor and I wanted to see people change. I wanted opportunities to speak to hurting souls and to point them to Jesus Christ, the one who provides for every need. Then I think of what's happened to me since my first book came out in late

2004. I've been all over the world. I've spoken to more people about Jesus since 2004 than all my previous years combined. I've received several thousand e-mails from strangers whose lives have been enriched because of the book.

Despite the physical reminders, God has enabled me to overcome the accident. And at times I also thank God for those handicaps—not because I want them, but because it means I can never forget the pain and despair I once felt. (Yes, I have wished God would remove my pain, and although that hasn't happened yet, I'm still eternally thankful to God.)

Recently I spoke to a group about overcoming. I said, "I overcame in Jesus' name, and he has been glorified. He deserves the praise. I supplied the busted-up legs and the gimpy arms, and he did the rest. That takes the burden off me, because I didn't do it. I'm an instrument and I like it that way. God knows what I can do and what I can't do. What gets done is what's important because I don't have the physical stamina to do everything."

I was a minister on my way to church when the accident happened. I was going to do something meaningful, which was to speak in church on a Wednesday night. I never did preach that sermon. My sermon on that following Sunday morning that never got preached was "I believe in a great God." I've always thought that was ironic but certainly poignant. Recently I preached a sermon with the same title, but the message was totally different. Today I preach about God's power, majesty, holiness, and glory. Those sermons were theological; today they're experiential. God has made the good so much better than the awfulness of the bad.

God, I pray that you will turn the pain and the trouble around so that my present life will become as good as it feels bad right now. I want to be surprised as I see you do far more than I could imagine. Thank you. Amen.

*When I refused to confess my sin, I was weak and
miserable, and I groaned all day long . . . Finally, I
confessed my sins to you and stopped trying to hide them.*

—PSALM 32: 3, 5*

65

"I'M SORRY"

"Dear Abby" once said that the two most difficult words
in English are, "I'm sorry." It's not easy for many of us
to admit that we're wrong or that we've failed.

Let's think a minute about what it means to admit that we're
wrong. Of course, we all want to be right. We want to know
everything, understand everything, and always operate with the
best of motives.

I've also learned that the more insecure we are and the less
we feel loved and valued, the more difficult it is for us to admit
our failures. We already feel bad and to admit failure makes us
even less significant.

To admit being wrong also acknowledges our humanness.
We face our imperfections. I think of the story of Adam and

Eve in Eden. After they realized they had sinned, they hid from God (as if they truly could). That's what happens to many of us when we realize our mistakes, shortcomings, and trespasses. We want to hide, to run away, or to do anything we can to avoid admitting we've failed.

As long as we can avoid accepting responsibility for our actions, we don't have to confess. It's easier to say, "But he said . . ." or "If you hadn't . . ." Of course, we pay the penalty for holding back on admitting our wrongs. As the psalmist said, "I was weak and miserable."

I stress this because I think many Christians live in misery because they won't or can't confess their wrongdoing. They'd rather suffer than admit they have sinned or failed. They hold grudges against others and are quick to say, "But she hurt me." She probably did. Our job is to forgive those who hurt us, and to go on with our lives.

When it comes to this topic of confession of sin, I often think of the powerful story Jesus told about a Pharisee (a religious leader) and a despised tax collector. (See Luke 18:9–14.) Luke introduced the story this way: "To some who were confident of their own righteousness and looked down on everybody else, Jesus told this parable" (Luke 18:9**).

The story is simple. The Pharisee stood and "prayed about himself" (Verse 11) and thanked God that he was righteous. The tax collector couldn't even look up and cried out, "God have mercy on me, a sinner" (Verse 13).

Jesus concluded the story, "I tell you that this man [the tax collector], rather than the other, went home justified . . ." (Verse 14).

It was the man who confessed—the tax collector—who found favor with Jesus.

Please know that God eagerly forgives our sins. John wrote these words: "If we say we have no sin, we are only fooling ourselves and refusing to accept the truth. But if we confess our sins to him, he is faithful and just to forgive us and to cleanse us from every wrong" (1 John 1:8–9*). That's the big hurdle: We need to admit our wrong and then confess to God. Once we open ourselves to God, we need to ask others to forgive us. That's the second step in the forgiveness process.

God of forgiveness, remind me that you love me so much there is nothing you can't and won't forgive. Help me to run to you for your loving mercy and forgiveness. And help me also to say to others, "I was wrong. I'm sorry." With your help I can do that. Amen.

*The earnest prayer of a righteous person has great power
and wonderful results.*

—James 5:16b[*]

66

EFFECTIVE PRAYER

I survived because of prayer.

I survived because one man felt God impress on him to pray for me, even though the EMTs said I was dead. He prayed anyway. He prayed me back to this earth. I returned, but no one knew if I would survive the next few days because my body had been so badly mangled. Thousands of people who heard about my accident prayed for me to survive after my return to earth. The word spread all over the country.

Again, I survived because of prayer.

During the time when others prayed for my recovery, I didn't—I couldn't. I wasn't sure I wanted to recover. I was ready for God to take me back to heaven—no, I was eager. I wanted to go back.

Eventually I reached the place where I prayed for a meaningful existence and for direction. My life had changed drastically and I was forced to depend on God for everything.

The depth and intensity of my prayer life increased. For those of us who have gone through those hard, painful, and life-changing events, we seek balance, and prayer becomes indispensable. As a result, it often becomes as natural to pray as it does to sing or talk.

I'm one of those people who needs God to write the words with a fingertip in the sky and to write in large letters. I'm not particularly perceptive about God's guidance. Despite that, I don't want to make a move without being certain what God has in mind for me. I ask him to make it absolutely clear to me. God usually does, and I'm grateful.

Not only did I survive because of prayer, but I also thrived because of prayer.

Prayer teaches us to think positively and if we learn to think positively, we also learn to act positively. But unless we aggressively pursue the new life—what I call the new normal—and work toward being positive about the outcome, we'll continue to struggle and bounce from highs to lows. If, however, we turn to positive prayer, we can become effective, and perhaps even more effective than we were before. We'll be different and we may be limited in some ways. There were things I could no longer do physically, but my life took on deeper, richer meaning.

After the accident I stopped being a youth minister and became a pastor to the entire church. For years, I had worked largely with the youth and I liked helping to shape their lives. I didn't make the change because I felt youth weren't worthy of my time, but because of my physical limitations I could no longer fulfill that role effectively. However, I have found meaning in my new role.

Through prayer I survived, I thrived, and my life was enriched. James says it this way: "The earnest prayer of a righteous person has great power and wonderful results." That says everything clearly. That kind of praying refers to more than an occasional crying out to God, but a daily, serious, committed, ongoing cry for God's guidance.

Another thing I learned: Prayer doesn't end with saying the words, but it becomes effective when we act on behalf of our prayers. When we pray, we also need to listen to God's response. Prayer, as the experts tell us, is conversation with God, not just a matter of piling up petitions and crying out about our needs.

We ask and we listen for God to answer, and then we act. One of my friends says, "We need to put legs on our prayers." That's action. It's not sitting and waiting for God to change us or our circumstances. If we hold back and keep saying, "I can't do that," we probably can't. That's why prayer is so powerful. Once we focus properly, we're ready for good things to happen in our lives.

Even after my release from the hospital, anyone who looked

at me might have thought, "That guy will never have any kind of meaningful existence again." They could have been correct. I could have given in and let everyone tell me what I could no longer do. The more I prayed, however, the more convinced I became that I needed to focus on what I *could* do.

I survived because of prayer.

I thrive because of prayer.

I grow because of prayer.

So can you.

Lord God of heaven, thank you for giving prayer as a powerful means of communication with you. Remind me that you care, that you want to hear from me, and that as I talk to you, you encourage and you change me. Remind me that faithful, committed prayers have great effect in this world. Don't let me forget that. Amen.

[Paul wrote] I was caught up into the third heaven fourteen years ago. Whether my body was there or just my spirit, I don't know; only God knows. But I do know that I was caught up into paradise and heard things so astounding that they cannot be told.

—2 CORINTHIANS 12:2–34*

67

HEAVEN AND BACK

I'm not the first person to go to heaven and come back. It's not that this is a common experience, but there may be more of such experiences of death and resuscitation than we know. One reason we don't have more accounts is because some people may not want to tell their stories.

Jesus' friend Lazarus died and was buried. Four days later, Jesus appeared at the tomb and shouted, " 'Lazarus, come out!' And Lazarus came out, bound in graveclothes, his face wrapped in a headcloth. Jesus told them, 'Unwrap him and let him go!' " (John 11:43–44*).

Lazarus died. There seems to be no question about that. So

where was he? The Bible doesn't say. In fact, the man is never mentioned after he walked out alive from the tomb. We don't know anything about him, but I believe my experience must have been somewhat similar to his.

In 2 Corinthians 11 and 12 Paul gives the most personal details of his life. He speaks about going into paradise or the third heaven. Wherever he went it was absolutely glorious, and then he came back. We don't know what happened to Paul, but one possible explanation appears in Acts. Paul and Barnabas preached in Lystra. Some antiChristian leaders stirred up the people "and turned the crowds into a murderous mob. They stoned Paul and dragged him out of the city, apparently dead. But as the believers stood around him, he got up and went back into the city . . ." (Acts 14:19b–20a*).

I want to point out two important things from that account. The crowd would certainly have made sure Paul had stopped breathing. They're called a murderous mob and that was the only way they could have been satisfied. Second, the Bible says Paul got up and went into the city. Apparently, he didn't go through a six-month period of recuperation. He got up and walked into the city. I can only conclude that was resuscitation and his personal statements in 2 Corinthians refer to that time.

And I think there are more people who have had this experience. I don't believe I am the only person who died, went to heaven, and returned. I am, however, the only one I know who has been willing to talk about his trip to heaven and back.

My experience took place in 1989 and fifteen years passed before I was ready to write about it. Had I wanted to capitalize on my story, would I have waited all those years before I wrote it? For most of those years, I did *not* want to revisit a very painful chapter of my life.

I believe God nudged me to speak up when I did and I see one significant purpose: When I speak, my words are to give hope and to offer encouragement. My death-to-life experience isn't meant to make me sound like a holy, special saint. My purpose is to say that heaven is wonderful and Jesus has a place ready and waiting for each of us. Just that. And all it takes for anyone to have eternal residence is to make a reservation through Jesus Christ.

My message is one of hope—a message to say that no matter how bad life may be on this earth, God lovingly erases all memories of pain and loss. When we enter the gates of heaven, we do so with nothing but perfect love, perfect peace, and perfect happiness forever.

That's worth looking forward to, isn't it?

God of heaven and earth, I don't understand many things about life and death, but I do understand that you have a place for me. I'm here to enjoy this life and to serve you. One day you will call me into my eternal home and I know it will be greater than anything I can possibly imagine. Thank you for that assurance. Amen.

. . . for Christ's sake, I delight in weaknesses, in insults,
in hardships, in persecutions, in difficulties.
For when I am weak, then I am strong.

—2 CORINTHIANS 12:10**

68
WHEN I'M WEAK

I like to feel strong, adequate, and capable. I like being complimented for the things I do for others, for my sermons, for my teachings, and being lauded for anything else that gets me praise. I'm human like everyone else.

I don't see anything wrong with that, but I've been thinking about Paul's words where he rejoiced in being weak. In the context of 2 Corinthians 12, the apostle wrote about his sufferings. After he cried for healing from his thorn in the flesh, God said his grace was enough for Paul's needs. The apostle then said that when he was weak he was really strong.

He obviously meant that once he stopped trying to handle everything himself, he had to depend on God. That's the real point: his total dependence on God. He never knew from day to day if he would survive. Most of us wouldn't want that kind of life, but Paul understood something few of us grasp: Whatever happened was all right because God was in full control.

Yes, we say those words, but Paul lived them. He knew that every day he had to depend on God just to survive. Most of us won't be in that kind of predicament, but he lived that way for years. And in the midst of that uncertainty about his circumstances, he found certainty in God.

To rejoice in his weakness didn't mean he wanted to be weak, ineffectual, and virtually useless. What he meant was he saw God's hand of grace at every point. When Jesus said his grace was sufficient, the apostle knew that God made up for his human deficiencies.

We want to be strong and to prove to the world how effective we can be; Paul wanted to be weak to prove to the world how effective God can be. As one of my friends used to say, "Why should God do anything for you that you can do for yourself?" The sufficiency of God's grace means that God intervenes when human endeavor is exhausted.

Paul's experience has been a source of deep blessing for God's people. He was a man who could be and was criticized and despised by many, he was a man with personal handicaps. Yet he was also a man filled with God's spirit. When he wrote, he did so out of his own personal agony and personal discovery. He was the man who could write, "But this precious treasure—this light and power that now shine within us—is held in perishable containers, that is, in our weak bodies. So everyone can see that our glorious power is from God and is not our own" (2 Corinthians 4:7*).

All-sufficient God, help me to depend more fully on you. Help me to realize that when I reach the end of my strength and deplete my resources, that's the moment you're ready to grab my hand and lift me up. You've done it before, but I forget so easily, so help me. Amen.

In his kindness God called you to his eternal glory by means of Jesus Christ. After you have suffered a little while, he will restore, support, and strengthen you, and he will place you on a firm foundation. All power is his forever and ever. Amen.

—1 Peter 5:10–11*

69

First the Suffering

No one wants to suffer. Peter understood that when he wrote to persecuted Christians. He emphasized the eternal glory. He wanted them to know the end of their journey would be glorious and eternal.

But he also had to say to them, "After you have suffered a little while, he will restore . . . you . . ." Although modern readers may not like that statement, to people already caught up in suffering, those were wonderful words of encouragement.

Peter wanted them to know it was "for a little while," even though it may have gone on for years. Compared to eternity with Jesus Christ, it truly is but a short time.

I wonder if believers of Peter's day and believers of our day need the same general message: Life isn't easy. The Bible never promises us that all will go smoothly or that we'll ever be problem-free. Instead, the Bible assures us of hardships and problems. Perhaps that's one reason the book of psalms provides comfort for many. I think of the countless times I've heard people tell me of the solace they've found in reading Psalm 23, 37, or 91. Some who struggle with sin and straightening out their lives resonate with David's vulnerability (and suffering) when they read Psalm 51. God provides the means to strengthen us; the psalms are there for us.

One of Job's friends may have been mistaken on a number of things, but he made one statement that speaks of the human situation. "For hardship does not spring from the soil, nor does trouble sprout from the ground. Yet human beings are born to trouble as surely as sparks fly upward" (Job 5:6–7[**]).

Even in those days, the wise understood a powerful truth: Suffering is a vital part of being alive; it's the price for citizenship in this world. We may not like it and we may groan and cry for help, but it's still part of being human.

I can't explain the reason for suffering or why God allows (or sends) it, but I've learned a couple of significant things since my own physical pain. Trauma, trouble, hardship, problems, or whatever we call adversity forces us to do at least two things. One is that we're forced to examine our lives. We may move into, "What's wrong with me?" or we might ask, "Why is everyone out to get me?" or "Why do people hate me?" No matter how we phrase the question, we look inward. If we do it well, in our search for answers, we also do the second thing: look upward. If life gets difficult enough, most of us look for some power, some strength beyond ourselves. "God, help me," becomes the natural cry. That's one of the most valuable possible outcomes I see for suffering.

Elsewhere, I've pointed out that pain and hardship change us. We're either hardened or we become more compassionate and tender. We become less judgmental and demanding of others because we want them to be kinder to us.

None of us likes to suffer; most of us will do whatever we can to avoid it. But Peter reminds us, "After you have suffered a little while, he will restore, support, and strengthen you, and he will place you on a firm foundation."

God, forgive me for complaining. Forgive me for trying to avoid the hard things I have to face, the serious issues I need to accept. Instead, remind me that these things will eventually pass. You have promised that after the suffering comes the joy and the happiness. Thank you for that promise and assurance. Amen.

*Have mercy on me, O God, according to your unfailing
love; according to your great compassion blot out my
transgressions . . . For I know my transgressions, and my
sin is always before me. Against you, you only,
have I sinned and done what is evil in your sight,
so that you are proved right when you speak and justified
when you judge . . . Surely you desire truth in the inner
parts; you teach me wisdom in the inmost place.*

—Psalm 51:1, 3–4, 6**

70

Truth in the Inner Being

I want to help people. I want to bring encouragement and urge people to open themselves to God. I don't want people to suffer and be in pain.

The one thing I feel I need to point out, and I do this reluctantly, is that sometimes our misfortunes and suffering are exactly what we deserve.

David understood that. Most of us know the story of his committing adultery with Bathsheba. He impregnated her, and then had her husband killed in battle so he could marry the woman. After the prophet Nathan exposed David's sin, the king cried out to God for mercy. We read the poignantly sad words of David in Psalm 51.

He not only confessed his sin, but he also saw something few of us seem to get: *Ultimately, all sin is against God.* It's God's laws we break. We hurt other people in the process (including ourselves) but we first offend our Creator and God. "Against you, you only, have I sinned and done what is evil in your sight," he wrote. David then went on to say, "so that you are proved right when you speak and justified when you judge."

David made no excuses for himself. He had committed adultery; he had deceived and lied; and he had murdered. We admire David because he accepted responsibility for his actions. It's true that he had to be confronted first, but once the prophet said to him, "You are the man!" David turned to God. (See 2 Samuel 12:7.**) The prophet pronounced punishment and here's David's response: "I have sinned against the Lord" (Verse 13). He took responsibility for his wrongdoing. He didn't blame Bathsheba's beguiling ways or refer to his impoverished childhood. "I did it. I'm guilty," he admitted.

That's one quality I see missing today. Too many Christians don't seem to realize that we have to take responsibility for our actions. We may have extenuating circumstances (and God knows), but the fact remains: We sin. We fail. And our sin starts with our failure to honor the laws of God.

When people talk to me, I don't urge them to confess their sin and I don't try to push them to reveal their failures. That's between them and God. But I wish—I truly wish—that I'd hear more people say, "I failed God and I've suffered. Now I want to get back on the right path and serve the Lord."

As much as I want to uplift, encourage, and bring a message of lasting hope, I also want to bring a message of self-examination. If we would take responsibility for our actions, we would avoid much of our suffering. And God is always eager to forgive.

When David faced his sin, he must have expected God to strike him dead, because the prophet said, "The Lord has taken away your sin. You are not going to die. But because by doing this you have made the enemies of the Lord show utter contempt, the son born to you will die" (Verse 13–14).

That's my final point: Like David and like all humans on this earth, when we sin we show utter contempt for the Lord. That means we despise him and his ways, even if only momentarily. It means we want our way so badly, we don't care what God wants. David never denied the truthfulness of that statement.

When life turns against us, it doesn't always mean we've sinned, but it's too easy to push aside our wrongdoing and focus on evil forces in the world, others' actions, or the low state of morals. Instead, we need to look inward and find truth in *our* inner being. God already knows; maybe we need to find out.

God, help me face myself; teach me to accept truth in my inner being. When I fail you, help me to see the enormity of my sin, even if it appears small to others. Enable me to see that you are the one I have offended. Then forgive me. Forgive me and lift up my head so I'll know I'm forgiven. Thank you. Amen.

Weeping may go on all night,
but joy comes with the morning.

—Psalm 30:5b, 6*

71

IS IT WORTH CARRYING ON?

In the first months after the release of *90 Minutes in Heaven*, I received almost seventy e-mails from people who told me that loved ones had taken their own lives. They were young, they were old; they were poor or wealthy; they were Caucasian, and people from dozens of other ethnic backgrounds. One woman wrote about her seventeen-year-old son. She sent his picture and told me what a wonderful boy he had been. He had been a basketball player and from all the outward evidence, he had everything going for him. But he took his own life.

After the deaths of those loved ones, the survivors often look back and say, "I should have noticed that."

Maybe. But often that's guilt nagging at them. That person made a decision and the survivors remain. That's one of the harsh realities of life. Those we lost may have been mentally ill, extremely angry, heavily depressed, or had profound secrets they couldn't talk about. Regardless of the reason, when people take their own lives, they leave behind hurting and devastated loved ones.

I know that none of us can do anything for those who have taken their lives, but we can do something for those who may be at that stage of despair. The one thing I've realized is that people who take their own lives feel hopeless. "There is nothing worth living for," they say. Their pain, whether physical or mental, feels so overwhelming they can think only of suicide to stop hurting.

As I've spoken around the country, I've realized that what seems hopeless tonight may not appear as bleak in the morning. I remember a time when I spoke to a woman late at night on the phone. She was desperate and was ready to take a fatal overdose of a prescription painkiller. I begged her, "Please, don't."

Despite my pleading, she seemed determined to take her own life. Finally, I said, "At least wait until morning. If you must take your life, a few hours shouldn't make much difference to you."

Reluctantly, she agreed to wait.

That night I prayed a lot for her. The next morning I called and she was still alive. She said, "Everything seemed so awful and hopeless last night, but today it's not quite as bad." She told me she had already called her pastor and a member of her church.

She realized, as the psalmist says, that the weeping goes on all night, but with morning things change. She had had time to reflect, and that gave her a reason to hold on. Maybe one of the rays of light was that she called me and I urged her not to give up. Maybe when she kept her promise and survived through the night, she also realized that there was hope for peace from her pain. Regardless of the reason, the morning was brighter than the darkness of the night.

As I write, I realize people have severe issues and maybe there's something about darkness that makes them seem worse. I know that if we can hold on a little longer, things change. God does love us and wants to come to our aid. Miracles may not happen immediately, but God does hear our cry and feels our pain with us.

God of comfort, sometimes I get so caught up in my own pain and problems that I forget that you never stop caring for me. Help me, dear God. Help me and remind me that joy does come in the morning. Amen.

Then Moses climbed Mount Nebo . . . There the Lord
showed him the whole land . . . Then the Lord said to
him, "This is the land I promised on oath to Abraham,
Isaac and Jacob . . . I have let you see it with your eyes,
but you will not cross over into it."

—DEUTERONOMY 34:1, 4[**]

72

IS GOD FAIR?

For forty years Moses put up with the bickering, groaning, and revolt of the people. They finally reached the end of the journey and were ready to go into the land but God wouldn't let Moses enter.

"How unfair can God be?" someone asked me. "If anyone deserved to cross the Jordan and go into the land it was Moses."

I didn't need to defend God's decision and I wouldn't know how. Sometimes we can see God's grand purposes, but not always.

It's easy to ask if God is fair when things don't go the way we want. It's easy to blame God when we don't get our way.

When tragedies strike, when life falls apart, when those whom we love desert us, it's easy to talk unfairness. And I don't have an explanation for any of those things. I do know, however, that it takes faith for us to grasp the reality that God is absolutely in control. It takes faith for us to accept that no matter what happens to us, to our loved ones, or to the world, God is sovereign and he isn't looking the other way.

When people raise questions about God being unfair, I understand them. They're not really saying that God isn't fair. They're saying, "I wanted something to happen and it didn't turn out the way I wanted." Or they say, "I didn't want this to happen and I don't deserve all this turmoil and pain."

They don't like their condition—whatever it is—and the easy solution is to complain about God's actions. That's how the Israelites did it. After God brought them out of Egypt and provided food for them, they didn't like what they received. He gave them manna, which was apparently a tasty, nutritious substance they found every morning on the ground. They wanted meat and melons. They wanted the food they had eaten in Egypt. "Is God fair to bring us out here and make us eat this horrible stuff?"

It's easy to call God unfair when his plan doesn't fit ours. All of us have those things in life that we didn't ask for, don't want, and wish they weren't in our lives. But they are the realities we have to face.

When an immediate and totally unexpected crisis strikes,

that's when we're most apt to ask such a question. But as Christians, we also know that God will get us through the immediate difficulties and losses. We know that the trauma we face now isn't for always. Like all of life, that, too, is temporary.

The only true answer I can offer is this: God loves us. God always does what's best for us. Sometimes divine action seems obvious, but not always. If we truly believe that we serve a God who loves us, we can cut through our pain and disappointment and affirm, "Yes, God is fair and just and always loving."

God, forgive me for the wrong questions I ask. Forgive me when I feel disappointed in what you do in my life. Help me to remember that you always work for my good and to make me more like Jesus Christ, and he suffered a painful, ignoble death. Amen.

. . . Do not use your freedom to indulge the sinful nature;
rather serve one another in love. The entire law is summed
up in a single command: "Love your neighbor as yourself."
—GALATIANS 5:13–14**

73
GETTING TOGETHER

I spoke to a woman right after her son had died and she, naturally, went through a period of intense grief. Occasionally, she e-mailed me or, in her darkest moments, phoned me.

One day she called and she talked so fast and with such excitement in her voice, I said, "Please slow down. I can't understand what you're saying."

She paused, took several deep breaths, and explained that she had gotten together a group of parents who had all lost children to suicide.

"Until I connected with others, I couldn't think about anyone else's grief. There truly are dozens of parents right here in our area just like me. They're people in grief and they felt the way I did—alone and desolate."

As I listened, I thought, *She doesn't sound like the same woman who first called me six months ago.* She was excited about her support group and excited that she had the opportunity to take her tragedy and do something that had meaning. She took her grief and turned it into something positive that could help others.

That's healing taking place, isn't it? I thought. That mother made a decision to look outside of herself. It was a deliberate choice to see the needs of others. The more she understood and felt their pain, the more healing it brought to her.

To reach outside ourselves is one of the greatest secrets of success. It's our opportunity to reach out and serve others. It's a way to say, "I've been there and I know the pain. I don't want anyone else to go through the same kind of devastating journey alone."

For most people, it's not an easy task to move outside their own grief. I don't mean to suggest a denial of the anguish and the trauma, but to go through the hurt and finally say, "Now I'm ready to move on. I'm ready to receive greater healing by being a means of helping others."

As soon as we can say, "I don't want to stay in this place. I don't want to live this way anymore," we are taking the first significant steps in our own healing.

That's the principle of Christian love, even if we don't realize it. Love, as presented in the Bible, isn't an emotion: It's an attitude. It's care put into action. That mother responded in love, or to use Paul's words, she used her freedom to serve others because "The entire law is summed up in a single command: 'Love your neighbor as yourself.'"

We don't have to heal anyone. We don't have to heal ourselves. What we need to do is to be open to compassion for others in pain. We need to see hurts where we can minister. When we can reach out to them and not be blinded or immobilized by our own situation, we can offer wonderful opportunities for their healing and for our own. That's fulfilling God's law.

Heavenly Father, it's often difficult for me to reach out to others. Some days I hurt too much to see beyond my own trauma, but I don't want to keep hurting. I don't want to live this pain-filled life anymore. Help me, by your loving, Holy Spirit, to be your instrument of healing for others. Amen.

Share each other's troubles and problems,
and in this way obey the law of Christ.

—GALATIANS 6:2*

74

"I DON'T WANT TO BE A BURDEN"

"I don't want to be a burden to anyone," the old man said. "I saved money and tried to provide for everything I'd need after I retired." His eyes watered and he pointed to his wheelchair. "But look at me! I can't even get out of this and into bed without help."

"If we live long enough," I said, "each of us will be a burden to someone, won't we?"

That conversation took place at least twenty years ago. If I could go back and change it, I'd say, "If we live long enough someone will take care of each of us." There is a difference between being cared for and being a burden.

Some people see their declining years as having to depend on someone else. Or because of an accident or illness, they can't do things for themselves and they have to have help. Too many people see that as totally negative.

"I've always been independent," one woman in the hospital complained. "It's difficult and maddening to me to lie here and wait for someone to empty my bed pan or bring my food."

Our culture hasn't always been like that. Cec lived in a so-called primitive section in East Africa for six years. In those days in Africa, the nationals had few of the modern conveniences such as flush toilets or electricity. Three or four generations of families often lived together. Parents cared for their children and their grandchildren and perhaps even their great-grandchildren. In many so-called primitive cultures, the day arrives when those caregivers become the care-receivers. They gave all through their adult lives, then it became their time to receive. No one objected; no one complained. That's the way it was.

In our culture, we assume that if people have to be inconvenienced or go out of their way to help us, we're a burden. We have so much to learn.

"Instead of thinking of ourselves as burdens," my friend Lydia said, "maybe we need to think of ourselves as blessings." She told me of her forty-one-year-old daughter. The daughter has never walked or ever spoken an intelligible sentence. But the family loves her. Lydia would have been offended if anyone had called her daughter a burden. "She is pure joy to be around."

We may understand this, but *we* don't want to be a problem.

We groan and resist surrendering control to someone else. Isn't it interesting that it's generally easier for caregivers to see the joy and the opportunity to help than it is for those who are helped? Those who often fear being a burden are lovingly cared for but they have difficulty in accepting that care. Instead of seeing only the negative side, maybe they need to see that they can also be a blessing to the caregivers.

During my extended hospital experience, I realized that whether I wanted to be a burden or not, I didn't have a choice. Sometimes God makes such choices for us. Sometimes we have to depend on others to survive. But then, that's how we started life, wasn't it? Maybe we need to see that depending on others is part of our lives until we leave this earth. Maybe we need to see that part of being in God's plan is that we spend many adult years giving care to our own children and perhaps to elderly relatives. But if we survive long enough, our time comes to get into the wheelchairs and the beds and be cared for. That's how life operates.

We all have instances when we need to be cared for. We all have those times when we fall and we can't get up by ourselves— literally or symbolically. In those moments we have to reach up and let someone take our hand and pull us to our feet. It may be a time of physical illness, emotional stress, or financial despair. The problem itself isn't as important as the realization that God is with us and uses other people to show divine compassion.

"Of course God is with us," a man snarled when I talked to

him about allowing others to care for him. He had been bed-ridden for almost a year.

"Do you consider yourself a burden to God?"

"Of course not."

"Do you feel you're a burden to God's children? To God's family?"

"Well, that's different," he said, but he got the message, even though it was still an adjustment for him.

Over the years I've heard sermons about Christians being God's human hands on this earth. We're God's heart for the hurting and we provide rest for the weary. If we ask our heavenly Father for help, is there any reason we can't ask God's Son, Jesus? Jesus won't think of us as burdens. If we can ask God's Son for help, is there anything wrong about asking God's other sons and daughters?

God, forgive me for being concerned about being a burden. Help me realize when I need a caring hand. Instead of resenting it, enable me to rejoice that there are those who can and will respond. And, God, as much as I'm able, help me to be your hands and heart to others. Amen.

*. . . Let us run with perseverance the race
marked out for us. Let us fix our eyes on Jesus, the author
and perfecter of our faith, who for the joy set before him
endured the cross, scorning its shame,
and sat down at the right hand of the throne of God.*

—HEBREWS 12:1B–2[**]

75

IT WILL BE BETTER

I still vividly remember a day when I did a book signing in Texas. The crowd was large and many bought books. Several people purchased multiple copies. At one point, I looked up and saw one man in a wheelchair with casts on both legs. He was pale and obviously in a lot of pain. His pallid complexion made it obvious he had been laid up a long time.

I sneaked glances at him several times while I signed books for other people. When he finally got to the head of the line, I smiled.

"I had my wife drive me here," he said.

"I'm so glad you came," I replied.

"We drove about two hundred miles." For a man with both legs in casts, that must have been a long and extremely painful ride.

"So what brought you here today?"

"I had to come to see you," he said. "I was in a car accident." His car had rolled over and because he wasn't wearing a seat belt he had been thrown from the vehicle. The accident mangled both his legs. Like me, he had been on a fixator. It had been removed only the week before.

"This week I'm going to start therapy."

"I'm going to be honest with you," I said. "Some of the worst pain is still ahead."

"I know."

No, you don't know, I thought. But the man was committed to endure. Even though he didn't know how much pain he had yet to face, I knew he would survive the ordeal.

Just before he left, the man said, "I don't know that I'm ever going to be able to go back and do the things that I used to do, the job I had before, but I'm looking forward to getting back on my feet and having a life." He paused and added, "Somehow though, I think my life is going to be better now than it was before—"

"Because?"

"Because I'm going to make it better. I'm going to work

at that. I've learned a lot about myself and I know it can be better."

As the man spoke, I thought of what Hebrews said about Jesus "who for the joy set before him endured . . ." I also thought of another statement: "Although he [Jesus] was a son, he learned obedience from what he suffered . . ." (Hebrew 5:8 **).

That's how the best part of life works. We suffer now, and in the midst of our pain we learn the price of following God's will. If we're open, we learn about ourselves and we become stronger and more mature. Sometimes I think God uses the hard places, the setbacks, and the disappointments to get our attention and say, "Okay, now you'll listen, won't you?" (I don't want to imply that every difficult situation is like that, but it was certainly true with me. We Christians need to realize that even our suffering can be therapeutic.)

I learned many lessons as I endured a total of thirty-four surgeries after my return to Earth. The single most significant lesson I learned is that I am a Christian who needs others. I had to be helpless before I admitted how much I needed to depend on others.

But I learned. *That's the best news.* Since then, I've become more sensitive to the need of people to serve me as I seek to serve others.

Lord, I don't like problems or pain or hardships. I don't like it when I'm not in control of my own body or my destiny. But I also know that I'm not really in control even during the best of times. You are the controller. Please enable me to recognize that and also to rejoice that you have a better plan for me than any of which I could ever conceive. Amen.

Teach us to number our days aright,
that we may gain a heart of wisdom.

—Psalm 90:12[**]

76

VALUING LIFE

Mary Thomas lay in hospice, in and out of consciousness. Each day, a staff member would say to her family, "Today is probably the day or surely tomorrow." Against all the medical knowledge, Mary kept breathing for twelve days, and that was at least ten more than anyone had expected.

"It's all right to let go," her son, Matt, said.

"You've made things right with God, with me, and with the family," her husband said.

Still Mary held on. One of the last things she said to her son was, "My life has been good."

Maybe that's why she held on so long: She valued her life now. Perhaps she didn't realize that the next stage of her life would not only be better, it would be perfect.

I admire people who value their lives, especially when they

overcome unbeatable odds. For example, at a book signing a woman said to me, "The doctors insisted I couldn't live, but I proved them wrong. Then they said I'd never walk again." She did a fancy little dance step for all of us. "See, I proved them wrong again."

We've read about the mountain climber Aron Ralston, who sawed off an arm to save his life. In an interview, he said, "I wanted to live." We know of people in the Siberian gulag or the Nazi concentration camps who survived for years on starvation diets. Others died around them, but they held on.

Most of us know stories like that. We admire their tenacity.

"How do they hold on when they should be dead?" I've heard that question asked many times.

My only answer is that these people value life. They want to live. I understand that refusal to give up. During my 108-day ordeal, and especially during my twelve days in ICU, there were times I groaned and cried out for God to take me. I meant those words, or perhaps because the pain was so overwhelming I thought life wasn't worth fighting for.

But I didn't quit. I held on, despite the pain, despite the prognosis. Deep within I wanted to live. From the divine perspective, of course, God wasn't ready to call me back permanently, but I wasn't able to think much about God's plan and purpose. I hurt and I wanted it to stop.

"Just let me die," I cried.

In retrospect, I really didn't want to die: I valued my life, even though it didn't seem as if I had much life ahead. Isn't that something God puts within us? Is it part of being human that many of us defy death sentences and survive amazing odds? What gave me the courage to keep on? I wouldn't have called it courage then, but I would today. It's the indomitable human spirit; we want life so badly we use all our resources not to lose it. As long as I hoped for a life with Eva and my children again, in my lucid moments, I believed the pain was worth it.

In other places, I've said that when hope is gone, we finally give up, but until we reach that point—until we're faced with that reality—we clutch at life. When I speak at churches I hear such stories. People share their experiences of endurance. They held on and beat the odds. They wanted to live.

I point this out because we need to understand that God gave us life and it's a gift. It's a gift for us to enjoy and to give thanks for every day we're on Earth.

I'm ready to make my final trip to heaven, but it's not my time. Until it is, I want to value my life. I want to honor God by my attitude and by the things I do. I travel a great deal and my body suffers. Some days I get off a plane and I can hardly walk. Some mornings I put on my shoes and my feet swell so badly that I can hardly take those shoes off my feet at night. Arthritis has crept all through my body and the pain continues to intensify. Some days it takes me a couple of hours to get my legs sufficiently loose so I can walk. At the end of long days I lie in bed and writhe in pain, trying to find a comfortable position so I can rest.

I can't give up. Not only do I value life as God's gift, but I believe God wants me to carry on faithfully until he finally calls me home—this time forever.

I'm not complaining. I am alive and I know that God has a purpose for keeping me alive. My desire is that when God finally calls me home, I'll hear Jesus say, "Well done, good and faithful servant."

Giver of life, remind me that I'm alive today because you have given me the gift of life. I'm alive and able to read this because you have chosen to give me at least one more day on earth. Help me to enjoy today and any other days that you may choose to give me before you call me to my heavenly home. Amen.

So it will be with the resurrection of the dead. The body
that is sown is perishable, it is raised imperishable;
it is sown in dishonor, it is raised in glory;
it is sown in weakness, it is raised in power;
it is sown a natural body, it is raised a spiritual body.

—1 CORINTHIANS 15:42–44A*

77

WE DIE THE SAME WAY WE LIVE

Many surgeons consider their work to be an art. Hours in the surgical suite often render patients miraculously better than they were before someone wheeled them into the operating room.

Someone criticized the work of one of the plastic surgeons who operated on me. "You could have done a better job of putting his left arm back together."

That remark highly offended the surgeon. He rebuked the offender and asked, "Were you there when they brought him into the operating room? Did you see what I had to work with? He had no bones, no muscles, and a huge gaping wound. That's one of the finest surgeries I've ever performed. It's a wonder that man even has an arm, much less one that functions as well as it does."

The doctor was right to take offense. Modern medical science can work miracles, yet some things can't be fixed. In my case it was a miracle; it just didn't look like a miracle.

By contrast, one of the cable channels devoted an hour-long program to celebrities and plastic surgery. An interesting note was that one minor celebrity gave a rather candid interview. Years earlier she had started with a simple nose job. A few months later, she decided to have a tummy tuck. "Then it became addictive," she said, and she spent thousands of dollars to make her body look better.

This isn't to rail against plastic surgery, Botox, or any cosmetic fix-up. But the program made it clear that those people identified with their bodies. One of them said, "I am my body. Why wouldn't I want it to be the best science can make it?"

My argument is that she is not her body. Her body is only part of who she is. It's an important, vital part, but only a part. I prefer to think of ourselves as spiritual beings who inhabit physical bodies.

When I went to heaven, I was so caught up in utter joy I didn't examine my body or stare at anyone else to see who looked stronger, healthier, or younger. I didn't notice eyeglasses or scars. Bodies didn't matter in heaven. Our bodies are here for us on earth, and they provide a covering for our spirits, but we survive long after our bodies have decayed.

The apostle Paul tried to make that point clear when he wrote to the Corinthians. Those believers had questions about what would happen when they died. Although they didn't have the same cosmetic concerns, they must have seen their bodies slipping away. Some had already died. Those still alive were getting older, grayer, slower, and less agile. As they aged, they must have wondered what lay ahead for them.

If they were nothing but bodies, the future would look bleak and desolate. That would have been the time to ask, "Is that all there is?" If, however, they saw that their bodies were like old models they would trade in for newer, perfect versions, they would have cause to rejoice. They could look forward to an endless life of no aches, no pain, no aging, and no need for plastic surgery.

If we accept that we are spirits, created by God, and that we live temporarily in an earthly container, we have no reason to fear wrinkles, baldness, or creaking joints. We have no reason to fear death. The spirit won't change. We'll remain who we are. And in heaven our new body will be perfect and never die or face corruption.

One Iraqi military veteran who had lost an arm and a leg told me, "I look toward the day when I'll be restored to perfect health." He also said, "For now, I know I'm connected with God. I'm ready to wait until that day of fulfillment."

That's the attitude all of us need: We look ahead for that perfection that comes to us when we reach our eternal home in heaven. My body looks like train tracks because of hundreds of stitches, staples, incisions, and skin grafts. But one day in heaven I'll be perfect. Jesus will be the only one with scars—and that's to remind us how we got there.

Creator God, thank you for making me who I am. Remind me that I inhabit a body, but my ultimate home is with you in heaven. Thank you that Jesus is there now and I have a special place set aside just for me. Amen.

But there is going to come a time of testing at the judgment day to see what kind of work each builder has done. Everyone's work will be put through the fire to see whether or not it keeps its value . . . if the work is burned up . . . The builders themselves will be saved, but like someone escaping through a wall of flames.

—1 CORINTHIANS 3:13, 15[*]

78

FACING JUDGMENT

In some denominations, they have a time of silence in their worship services where people confess their sins before the pastor prays aloud for everyone and closes by saying something such as, "In the name of Jesus Christ, I declare to you that our sins are forgiven." He isn't offering them forgiveness but is only declaring what the Bible teaches. He is saying that because they have confessed their sins, they have been forgiven.

Those pastors try to make it clear that Jesus Christ is in the forgiving business. If we love him and confess our transgressions, we're forgiven.

Despite that, many people lack assurance of God's forgiveness. Even though they openly acknowledge their faith in Jesus Christ as their Savior, have heard that their sins are wiped away, and have read about absolution in the Bible, they fear they'll have to face some terrible judgment or feel there are horrible things they've done that God can't forget or erase.

At one time, probably every pastor has heard someone say, "I've done something too wicked for God's mercy to overcome." What they usually mean is that they can't *feel* that they're worth being loved and accepted by God. But God never created anyone too evil to be loved. The Bible makes it so clear that if we turn to him, the gift of salvation includes God's acceptance of us as we are and that acceptance also involves forgiving our sins.

This makes me wonder if some people feel God's forgiveness only stretches to a point and then the Lord says, "No more," or "I've erased too many sins too many times already and you've exceeded the limit."

This isn't a logical or intellectual issue. If we say to anyone, "Do you *believe* that God has wiped away every sin?" the answer is yes. But if we ask, "Do you *feel* as if you're forgiven? Do you feel that in the life ahead God will punish you?" That's when we hear contradictory answers.

For many, not feeling forgiven is the same as not being forgiven. They are unable to recognize that their feelings are emotions and not reality. Their own sense of worthlessness or their lack of self-esteem hinders them from enjoying life now and receiving hope and peace as they face their eternal future.

I want to continue to assure them and to explain that there is a judgment for Christians. But it's not a judgment that results in punishment. God's judgment is to reward us for our service. Although all Christians go to heaven, the Bible makes it clear that our rewards will vary. Some will receive great honor, others small, and Paul makes it clear that some will make it inside the gate, but have no reward for their behavior.

Paul didn't want the Corinthian readers to think they'd been discarded or pushed away by God. He did want them to realize that even though they would make it to heaven, God would examine their lives and reward them according to their deeds. That makes sense, doesn't it?

If we're faithful in serving God, we're rewarded well; if we're only partially faithful, God rewards us accordingly. Regardless, if we belong to God, heaven will be our final residence. Paul said it this way, "So now there is no condemnation for those who belong to Christ Jesus" (Romans 8:1**).

Just and loving God, I belong to you and you know my motives as well as my actions. Help both of them to please you at all times. Remind me that there is no future punishment for me because I'm your child. Amen.

[God] has identified us as his own by placing
the Holy Spirit in our hearts as the first install-
ment of everything he will give us.

—2 Corinthians 1:22[*]

79

What She Never Had in Life

A woman who identified herself only as Millie from Virginia e-mailed me about a month after her mother died. She said that her grown son came for the funeral and had brought a copy of *90 Minutes in Heaven*. Millie was able to read the book before the funeral.

Millie wrote that even though her mother believed in God, she was a very unhappy person all through her life. However, after reading my book she felt her mother was finally able to achieve some peace.

"Reading your story made me realize once again that, at last, she can have what she never had in this life." This realization helped her in her grief, knowing that her mother was finally happy.

I liked those words: "She can have what she never had in this life." That's true for all of us. In this life, we all have bad times. Stress, sickness, disappointments, and heartaches. Most of us, especially if we're Christians, would also say that we've had more good times than bad.

Part of our expectation is that in heaven we'll experience in fullness what we've felt only in small measure here on Earth. We can trust that the best is yet to be. The proof we have, in the words of the apostle Paul, is that God has given us the Holy Spirit as a token or a down payment. It's like earnest money in a real estate deal. The gift of the Holy Spirit is like writing us a promissory note for fulfillment when we reach the gates of heaven.

As I thought of that verse and Millie's mother, I felt sad. Without meaning to judge, her mother sounded like others I've met. They have the spiritual resources available just as we do. The difference is that they choose not to take advantage of what they have and, consequently, they don't enjoy their lives.

By nature, some people are more melancholic, but if we have the Holy Spirit as God's down payment of eternal joy and perfect love, how can we honor God if we don't take advantage of such grace? In fact, if we live with a negative attitude isn't that living far below the life God wants for us? Despite our nature, we have no excuse for not living the fulfilled or abundant life that Jesus promised. Whatever we need is available.

Like Millie, I believe her mother will have what she never

had in this life. She will know the "joy unspeakable and full of glory" that comes only in heaven. But she could have been so much happier if she had said yes to God's resources while she was alive.

At times, all of us have down times and even moments of despair, but we don't have to stay down. That's the difference between us and those who never know the true joy of the Christian experience.

Dear Holy Spirit, thank you for being in my life. Help me to accept your gifts and encouragement. Remind me that you can help me make my life on Earth a foretaste of the glory of heaven. Amen.

[Jesus said,] "Unless you are faithful in small matters,
you won't be faithful in large ones."

—LUKE 16:10*

80

FAITHFUL IN LITTLE;
FAITHFUL IN MUCH

I felt honored to be invited to share the story of *90 Minutes in Heaven* with a church where I had once been the youth minister. After I arrived, a number of people greeted me. Most of them had been teens when I left and now they were in their thirties and forties. They proudly brought their families to meet me and told me of their vocations. Some of their children were as old as they themselves had been when they were members of my youth group.

After I had preached in the morning services, someone escorted me to a book-signing table in the foyer. That turned out to be a blessed reunion with many of my former parishioners. As I greeted countless old friends, I looked up to see a tall, handsome young man in his thirties, and he smiled at me. Even though I remembered him from the youth group, I had forgotten his name.

"I'm Zane."

Then I remembered. Zane Nipper had been an incredible baseball player and an exceptional young man in our youth group. Floods of memories filled in the blank spots as I shook his hand. He introduced me to his beautiful wife and his two good-looking children. God had obviously favored him. We talked about the old days.

"It was great, wasn't it?" Zane said. "It means so much to me to see you again."

"Yes, it was a blessed time. I'm so proud for you. You have a wonderful family and have become a fine young man, just as I knew you would."

I signed a book for them and the crush of the crowd moved them along. I caught sight of him out of the corner of my eye just before the Nippers exited, and I smiled and waved at his sweet kids. I turned my attention back to the ever-moving line of well-wishers.

About a minute later, I felt someone touch my left shoulder. As I turned to see who it was, a man laid his head on my shoulder.

Bending his six-foot-four-inch frame over me was Zane. "You'll never know what you mean to me," he said.

I stretched my gimpy left arm around to embrace him. He kept his head on my shoulder, and his tears ran down my neck.

"Zane, brother, bless you. You and the other young people

of this church meant so much more to me than I could ever say. I love you."

Zane nodded and wrapped his large arms around me.

"I hope to see you again this side of heaven, my friend," I said.

"I'd like that very much." He turned and smiled with utter sincerity.

"Me, too," I said.

Almost immediately he pulled away and disappeared into the crowd. I turned back to the others in line, but I couldn't shake that heartfelt moment with Zane.

Later in my car on the way home, I reflected on that amazing encounter. Not only does my present ministry matter since I've returned from heaven, I thought, but even what I did before the wreck matters. And it will always matter. God used my life and my testimony about my death and resuscitation, but I also realized something else. I had tried to be faithful to God long before the accident. It's easy to think of my significant ministry beginning after the publication of my first book, but Zane brought home a powerful truth to me: It all matters. Whatever we do, God counts it as service.

I had no idea that my ministry to Zane twenty years ago would have that kind of impact on his life. How could I have known? How could we know about dozens of things we do today that pay off in the future? The only thing I know is this: If we're faithful now, we'll be rewarded in the future. Our rewards may be as simple as those poignant moments of a big guy hugging me, crying, and telling me how much I had impacted his life.

Although I finally remembered Zane, I truly wasn't aware of any significant role I had played in his life. For a moment as I listened to him, I wished I had been more aware, but afterward I thought, "That's also how God works, isn't it?" We do what we can when we can. We do the right things because they're right and because we have the opportunities and the ability to do them.

Paul encouraged early Christians with these words: ". . . Be strong and steady, always enthusiastic about the Lord's work, for you know that nothing you do for the Lord is ever useless" (1 Corinthians 15:58*).

Then once in a while—not often, but once in a while—a Zane walks up to us, hugs us, and we know we haven't served God in vain.

Faithful God, teach me to be faithful to you in everything, and especially in the things that I don't consider important or would prefer not to do. Everything is important to you and I want to be faithful in every task you give me. Thank you for helping me to realize this. Amen.

*To him who overcomes, I will give the right to eat
from the tree of life, which is in the paradise of God.*
—REVELATION 2:7**

81
THE OVERCOMERS

The man sheepishly walked over to the book table, and he was the last one in line. He leaned over and said, "I've been a Christian for more than twenty years, but I'm a failure." His voice cracked as he talked about his failures. "By now I should be a real overcomer. I know the right things to do, but I—well, I just don't always do them. Sometimes I deliberately do hurtful things. What kind of Christian am I?"

"Probably a growing Christian," I said and smiled. I'm sure he expected a rebuke, and I began to explain that I hadn't misunderstood his words.

"I heard you," I said. "Has it occurred to you that if you weren't growing you wouldn't feel bad about your failures? If you weren't growing, you'd probably stand here and tell me about how good you are and how grateful God must be to have you on his side. Or maybe you wouldn't even be here."

"But I fail God many times."

"I heard you and I'm sure that's true. You fail, and you fail a lot. That's something most of us are good at doing." I leaned forward and asked, "Do you know any perfect Christians?"

"No, of course not, but—"

"So if they're not perfect, that means they fail. Think about it: Even one lapse still means they are less than perfect."

That encounter helped me to realize that we can only do our best. And God loves us even when we're fallible and imperfect.

None of us is perfect. Even after my brief trip to heaven, I'm still a weak, fallible creature. We beat up on ourselves endlessly for being sinful and imperfect. When we do, we feel bad and may even want to give up. That's not the message of the Holy Spirit. God doesn't want us to become discouraged or quit. God wants us to overcome.

In John's book of Revelation, he sent letters to seven churches. To each of them he wrote, "He who overcomes . . ." and pronounced a promise. We love those promises and most of us truly want to be overcomers.

If we read those seven letters John wrote, most of them contain a rebuke (and the last one is a scorcher), but the purpose is to exhort them to keep fighting and to overcome every obstacle.

If we dwell on what we haven't done, or concentrate on why

we should be more spiritual or focus on how spiritual we ought to be, if we think of our defects and shortcomings, we're going to lose. We're going to be overcome instead of overcoming.

That man who moaned about his failure was probably a much healthier Christian than he realized. He seemed to think that holy, victorious living came from one major victory after another and a cessation of struggles. Most of us have our times of spiritual breakthrough; however, most of our victories come slowly and we seem to inch forward. Or maybe we move so slowly we're not aware that it's forward motion. That may have been his trouble: Maybe he expected one quick leap from abject sinner to overcoming Christian.

Because we move slowly in our spiritual growth, we're often unaware how far we've traveled. Life is a struggle and spiritual forces work against us. We're human and we make bad choices and slip off the path. We don't ever reach the place where we don't have to fight to be victorious. We also need to remember, it's not just our personal fight. Jesus Christ is with us and fights for us. If we call on him he rushes to strengthen us and to urge us onward. "To him who overcomes . . ."

I said one more thing to the man at the table. "You've failed, but you've also succeeded. You've stood your ground. You've made progress. You're on your way to a fuller, more lasting victory."

He smiled and shook my hand. "That's the encouragement I needed."

Dear God, when I remind myself of my failures, please remind me of the victories. When I want to give up, remind me that you love me enough that you won't let me quit. Continue to fill me with hope; continue to remind me that you are the only totally victorious one. I want to be more and more like you. Amen.

The Lord appeared to us in the past, saying:
"I have loved you with an everlasting love;
I have drawn you with unfailing kindness."

—JEREMIAH 31:3***

82

THE MEANING OF LIFE

"What is the meaning of life?"

Someone asked me that question. Perhaps because of my death and resuscitation he felt I had figured out all the answers. Instead I looked him in the eyes and said, "I have no idea. Besides that, I can't answer the question in the abstract, but I can tell you about the meaning of *my* life."

We didn't discuss it further, but if we had I would have told him, "I don't want to focus on some objective, abstract concept of life, because I want to know the purpose and the meaning of my life."

Isn't that what all of us yearn for?

Each of us has a vocation, a calling, talents, and our responsibility is to see how they fit into God's plan for our lives. I like to think that each of us has a divine assignment in life. God calls us permanently home when we have completed that assignment, and only he knows when that assignment is fulfilled.

When anyone wants to ask about life in general, I always come back to my life and how I live it. That's where I'm the expert. That also means two things.

First, I have to figure out what God wants me to do with my life. God doesn't lay out a plan for any of us to read and memorize, but it's a plan that unfolds only in obedience. The best illustration I can think of how that works is to refer to the time when the Israelites reached the Jordan River and were ready to cross into the Promised Land. The story is found in Joshua Chapter 3. The priests carried the Ark of the Covenant and led the people forward. Joshua recorded it: "Now the Jordan is at flood stage all during harvest. Yet as soon as the priests who carried the ark reached the Jordan and their feet touched the water's edge, the water from upstream stopped flowing. It piled up in a heap a great distance away . . ." (Joshua 3:15–16***). The account tells us that the priests stood in the middle of the river until the people passed to the other side.

The point of the story is that the river didn't stop flowing until the priests reached the edge of the water. They had to be in place before God started the action. That's how life works: We do what we know to do and then God shows us the next step.

Second, my life has value even if I don't always seem aware of that fact. I have a place, a purpose, and a calling. Sometimes

God lets me walk in darkness for a while. Sometimes I seem to have no sense of God's presence—and I've been there, especially in the months after my accident. But life still has meaning. I may not know the meaning of life in general or even the meaning of my own life, but I do know the Giver of life. That's even more important.

God, my life has meaning because you have given it meaning. My life has value because you love me. When I have those dark days, remind me that I am loved by you. Sometimes I forget, so keep on reminding me. Amen.

Remember that in a race everyone runs, but only one person
gets the prize. You also must run in such a way that you
will win. All athletes practice strict self-control.
They do it to win a prize that will fade away,
but we do it for an eternal prize.

—1 Corinthians 9:24–25*

83

Running the Race

"Of course I'm depressed," she said to me. "If you had my kind of troubles, you'd be depressed too." Before I could say anything more she vented all her anger, but she never raised the volume. Her dead eyes stared at me and she sounded like some kind of zombie reciting by rote.

When she paused, I asked, "What good things are you doing for yourself?"

She stared at me as if to ask, "What *good* things?"

One of the biggest signs of depression I see in people is that they have stopped doing the things they once enjoyed. When

I asked the woman, she said, "Nothing. It just takes too much effort."

"Do you go to church or have fellowship with other Christians?"

"I don't fit with any of them."

I kept urging her to think of something she enjoyed and finally she said, "I'm so miserable, I don't know what I enjoy doing."

Her daughter stood next to her and said, "Mama, you used to like to knit. You made such beautiful sweaters—"

"Who cares about sweaters?" she said in that dull voice.

"You *used* to," I said.

We talked for several more minutes and nothing much changed, but I like to think I gave her a few things to think about. She was on heavy medication, which probably made her feel "worthless, ugly, and unloved" (her words).

What I hope depressed people will grasp is that they can get help. Beyond the medical answers, we also know that faith in Jesus Christ lifts many out of despair. But to push out of depression means they have to do some things for themselves.

The people who seem the most troubled are those who can't accept the changes in their lives. They're angry at what has happened and they won't accept it. "I didn't deserve all the stuff that's happened to me," one man said.

"You're right," I said. "That's a valid point, but it doesn't change anything. Life isn't fair. Bad things often happen to good people. So what are you going to do about it?"

He stared at me in confusion. Until that moment, it was obvious he hadn't asked himself that question.

In recent years, we've had war in the Middle East, a tsunami in the South Pacific, devastating hurricanes on America's Gulf Coast, earthquakes in Pakistan, and famine in Africa. The list goes on endlessly. That's out there and it's sad news, but it doesn't directly affect most of us. But then someone we love is severely injured in a car wreck. We have a death in the family. Our company goes bankrupt and we lose our jobs. Our lovely daughter or handsome son has turned to drugs.

Life—hard life—hits us all at some point. It's not that we have to embrace these things and keep our minds focused on them every day and every hour of the day. It's that we accept them and decide what we need to do next. We have to decide that we won't be overcome, defeated, and knocked completely out of the race.

Running the race is an image Paul used in writing to the Corinthians. I like that image because life is like a race. Some run faster than others, but it's still a race. To win, we have to stay in it until we reach the finish line. We can't drop out at midpoint, but we must endure, pant, wheeze, groan, and keep on running. That's the secret (if there is one): We endure.

Sometimes simply enduring is the hardest part. It's also a big test for us. Just to keep moving is all we can do, but as long as we keep moving, we're still in the race.

Life may never get easier and the pain may increase. My body hurts worse these days than it ever has. Some days it would be easier for me to say, "I'm through. I give up." But I can't do that. I'm still in the race.

We can all run—no matter how slowly. Paul reminds us that our prize is an eternal one. We have so much waiting for us. And here's what thrills me most: I envision Jesus, Paul, Peter, and all the saints standing at the finish line and cheering for me. "You can make it. Just a little farther," they shout to me.

With that kind of encouragement, I know I can make it!

Dear God, sometimes the race seems hardly worth the effort. I feel depressed or worn out and I wonder if I even want to make it. But it is worth the effort. Keep reminding me. And thank you that Jesus leads the cheering section for me. Amen.

Consider it pure joy, my brothers and sisters,
when you face trials of many kinds, because you know
that the testing of your faith produces perseverance.
Let perseverance finish its work so that you may be
mature and complete, not lacking anything.

—James 1:2–4***

84

PERFECTION OF PATIENCE

Some Bibles translate the Greek word *makrothumeo* as patience and others as endurance. Regardless of how the scholars translate it, the word isn't a characteristic most of us have naturally. It's a learned element in our lives, and we don't learn it by thinking or reading about *makrothumeo*. It comes from experience, and often experience that is difficult and painful.

It hasn't been easy for me to embrace patience. Even now, years after my accident, I vividly remember when the hospital staff came to get me on a gurney and take me to physical therapy. I *especially* remember when they set the table up that I was on and forced me to stand upright for the first time in weeks. I became nauseous and incredibly sick because my equilibrium had totally rearranged itself. I couldn't handle the drastic change in my physical position. It was a very painful, very slow process to learn how to walk again.

Because my arm had been so badly injured, I had a red rubber ball that they gave me to squeeze. I didn't like squeezing that tiny thing because it hurt. But I did what I had to do. I learned to stay with it—to endure—regardless of the pain.

When I lay in the ICU with pneumonia, the doctor came in and badgered me into breathing into the machine to try to get my lungs cleared up. I wasn't patient then and I was angry because it hurt to take deep breaths. I wanted to have everything over with. I wanted to breathe on my own without pain. I wanted to be able to use my arm again. I wanted to walk on my own; so I did what they told me, even though I did everything with reluctance.

I'd had massive surgery and I wanted to skip over the therapy and just feel good again. It doesn't work that way. We have to "earn" the right to feel good again by going through the ordeal of persevering through the hurting times.

I got out of the hospital, of course, but first I had to learn to endure the pain. Patience is absolutely critical. If we don't develop the ability to hold on and keep fighting, we just don't make it. I've known people who have had massive surgeries and want to skip the therapy. It doesn't work that way. We have to work hard to feel good again. Enduring the ordeal of therapy and recovery often means persevering through hard, hurting times.

There's the famous illustration about the person who saw the caterpillar about to change into a butterfly. The creature struggled to get out of the chrysalis. The would-be-helpful person removed the butterfly to stop the painful ordeal. He got the butterfly out but it could never fly. The struggle makes butterflies able to fly. Enduring the slow, painful hardship allows endurance to develop. We may not like the ordeals we face, but if we're going to soar (or even survive), we have to go through those times.

We also have to do it at the right time—not too early and not too late. And most of all, we have to be kind to ourselves and not get frustrated over our lack of patience. Those who are committed to living the easy way miss this important ingredient of a good life: The struggles make us stronger. James exhorts us to count those difficult times as periods of joy. They may not seem joyful at the time, but they show us that we're making progress. We don't go backward and we progress. We become stronger and able to handle the next trauma that comes our way because we know we handled the last one.

Isn't that an excellent reason for joy?

God, forgive me for wanting to bypass the hard places. Remind me that you made me and you gave me the capacity for endurance. Enable me to rely on you to help me through those tough places. Amen.

*Our days on earth are like grass; like wildflowers,
we bloom and die. The wind blows, and we are gone—
as though we had never been here. But the love of the
Lord remains forever with those who fear him.*

—PSALM 103:15–17*

85

FEARING DEATH

"So you're not afraid to die?" That's one of the questions a radio talk show host asked.

"No. I don't know that I ever particularly feared death," I said. "I've never thought myself to be a particularly fearful person."

He didn't pursue the topic, but I think he hit on something significant: Many people (maybe most) fear death, and for a variety of reasons. I understand why people might fear death. It's an unknown process. It's uncertain and it's irrevocable. I understand that, but based on my experience it didn't actually turn out to be irrevocable, because I've had a temporary reprieve.

It is not unknown to me because I died and returned to life. No, I'm not the least bit fearful about the end of existence on this earth.

People have a tendency to think this is it—this life now—and they live that way. They really live to maximize their time on earth. I understand that. I think we ought to make the most of life right now. Let's enjoy today and every day. But we ought to live our time with the knowledge that this life is temporary. Only heaven is permanent. We need to live in such a way that when we come to the end of our earthly existence, we can smile and say, "I've spent my whole life in preparation for this moment. I'm ready for the joyful perfection that's ahead."

Perhaps we don't want to think that far ahead. Some all but deny death. "That's such a depressing subject," people have said to me. It really isn't, but it becomes depressing to those who don't want to face the reality of the future and of their own demise.

I don't know all the reasons people fear death, but I've thought of a few of them.

"Those of us who most fully welcome life will welcome death as well," said a pastor at a funeral. He talked about a vivacious woman who died in an accident at age eighty-six.

Too many people run away from death, and that means they also flee their own lives. By that, I mean, they're withdrawn, consumed with guilt, too dependent, too independent, too ambitious, too ashamed, or too proud. They don't have any deep-felt joy or peace now. How can they look forward to something they haven't begun to experience here? Because they can't face their lives joyfully now, they can't face their deaths peacefully.

Some are afraid because of the lack of quality of their involvement with others. That is, their deaths are a problem because their daily living is a problem. If we fear to interact with others now, we also fear death. Here's a strange paradox but I believe it: The more fully we enjoy our life on earth and our relationships, the more prepared we are for eternity. The psalmist reminds us that our presence on earth is short and we're like flowers that bloom, die, then they're gone and never remembered. As humans, not many of us will be remembered on this earth for more than a couple of generations.

The joy of eternal life is that there is no ending, no parting, no struggling, and no suffering. If we think of death as graduation, that may help. At the end of high school or college we have a *commencement* ceremony. We are embarking on a new phase of our life that will be better and more fulfilling because we're more fitted to cope with what lies ahead. That's how we should approach death: by being prepared to commence a new stage of life.

We may never be remembered here, but we're never forgotten *there* because Jesus promised that he has places prepared for us. *Prepared for us!* That means it's no accident or just luck. It's all set up and our special place awaits our coming.

Afraid of death? Not me. I know what happens next.

God, take away any fear of death I have. Help me know that death is not the end, but only the necessary step to go through before I enjoy your presence forever and ever. Amen.

"O death, where is your victory? O death, where is your sting?" For sin is the sting that results in death, and the law gives sin its power. How we thank God, who gives us victory over sin and death through Jesus Christ our Lord!

—1 Corinthians 15:55–57[*]

86

WHAT FOLLOWS DEATH

He hovered over me at a book signing but kept motioning for other people to move in front of him. When no one else remained, he leaned close and said, "I'm a Christian, but I'm afraid to die."

I've learned not to show any shock no matter what anyone says. I stared at him and waited for him to continue.

"It's not so much dying, but I'm afraid of what comes after that. You know, the unknown. I have that sense of nothing but darkness between dying and getting to heaven."

I tried to assure him that there is no dark passage. "One minute you're on earth and the next conscious moment you're meeting the welcome committee at the gate." I spoke of the blessings of heaven and the perfection, but the man seemed to find no peace.

He talked to me for perhaps twenty minutes and practically told me his entire life story. No matter what I said, the man seemed uneasy. "I know it sounds silly, but I'm afraid. I believe, but—"

Finally the man walked away. He still hadn't resolved his fear of dying. As I reflected on the conversation and the things the man said, understanding seeped into my mind.

From what he told me, I felt I had a fairly good picture of who he was. He's always played life safe, I thought. The man had made it plain that he had never taken risks, had never moved out of his hometown, had taken the first job offered him after high school, and had remained in it for nearly thirty years.

He's afraid of life.

Why wouldn't he be afraid of death?

As I pondered that thought, I understood. The people who fear what comes after death are often those who can't face the unknown today. They are too timid to enjoy the "right now" in their lives. If they're afraid of risks, of trying anything new, or of exploring possibilities, it's no wonder they're afraid of dying. They seem able to conceive only of nothingness—and they're afraid of nothingness.

In fact, in recent years, experts have invented a term for that kind of fear: neophobia, the fear of new experiences. A study at the University of Chicago released in 2003 suggests that a lifetime of fearful stress takes an accumulated toll on our health. Fearful people tend not to live as long.

Aside from the possibilities of a shorter life, it's sad that fearful people have a life without deep joy and peace. How can they possibly enjoy now if they focus their attention on tomorrow's dark clouds? Jesus said, "So don't worry about tomorrow, for tomorrow will bring its own worries" (Matthew 6:34a*).

I wish that man had been able to focus on the joy now and not fear what came next. But why wouldn't he be afraid? He's been afraid all his life.

God of peace and joy, help me live life today to the fullest. Despite my troubles and problems, remind me that you are in control and that I truly have nothing to fear. You're with me. May your presence take away all my worries and fears. Amen.

He [God] will wipe every tear from their eyes.
There will be no more death or mourning
or crying or pain . . .
—Revelation 21:4**

87

No More Sorrow

Like many others who felt they needed to talk to me personally, the middle-aged woman stood back from the crowd and waited. As soon as the number of people thinned, she walked over to me.

And also like many others, she had to fight back tears when she talked. She told me about her husband's lingering illness from cancer and congestive heart failure. For more than a month, he lay in bed and was kept alive by IVs and a supply of oxygen. The medical staff had made him well aware that he had no chance of recovery.

"Over the years of our marriage, I tried to talk to him about surrendering his life to Jesus Christ," she said, "but he never listened." For several minutes she detailed their years together and his refusal to go to church with her or to listen to anyone talk about Jesus Christ.

"When he was diagnosed with lung cancer," she said, "I was sure he'd open himself to God and see his need." He didn't.

The husband had been a smoker for more than forty years and the diagnosis came too late for him to recover. She prayed for him daily; members of her church prayed; the minister visited several times. Others sent books and pamphlets. Nothing changed him. He wasn't rude or angry, but would say simply, "I'm not interested."

"He died without Jesus Christ," she said. Her resolve broke and the tears came. Someone who stood nearby offered her a tissue. "I loved my husband and I break down and cry whenever I realize that I'll be in God's wonderful presence and he won't be."

I waited until she had quieted before I leaned closer. "Heaven is a perfect place and—"

"I know and that's why I'm so broken up."

"I'm not sure what you mean," I said.

"I'll be there and he won't be. How can I be happy when I'll think of him all the time?"

"Heaven is a place of perfect happiness," I said again. "While we're on this earth, we grieve over those who refuse to surrender themselves to God. That's natural. We want the best for them and—"

"Yes, that's it exactly—"

"Heaven is a place of perfect happiness," I said for the third time. "You rejoice. You rejoice in those who are with you, but you have no memories of those who are not."

She stared at him. "But how is that possible?"

"I can tell you only that heaven is perfect. You believe that, don't you?"

She nodded.

"Then also believe that God wipes away and totally erases everything that isn't perfect." I smiled then and asked, "Have you ever sinned?"

When she said that of course she had, I pointed out, "When you get to heaven, do you expect to remember those sins? If you still remember your failures, it won't be a perfect place."

"Oh, that's right." She understood and her face radiated joy.

As I've spoken to people around the world, many people live in fear of the future (even believers) because they don't understand. Heaven is a place of complete, total, and utter happiness, peace, and joy. I assure my audiences that there is no sorrow in heaven. There will be no regrets, no looking back, and no one will ever say, "If only I had not . . ."

The Book of Revelation promises us that God will wipe away our tears. That symbolic language is God's promise that we'll have no unpleasant memories, no haunting secrets, and no tormenting questions.

How can it be otherwise? Heaven is a place of perfect happiness.

Great God of love, remind me again and again that heaven means total happiness. I'll have no tears there, no failures to report, and no sins to confess. Because you are there and I'm with you, everything will be perfect. Amen.

[Jesus said,] "You know the way to the place where I am going . . . I am the way and the truth and the life. No one comes to the Father except through me."

—John 14:4, 6**

88
Why Am I Here?

Among the scores of e-mails I receive daily, there is one question I get four or five times each week. The question usually comes from parents who have a child or a relative that committed suicide.

"Did he go to heaven?"

The only way I can respond is to ask about the spiritual attitude of that person. Where was the person spiritually? I refuse to give false assurance. False hope is not true hope.

As I've thought about this, I understand the dilemma and the concern of those who have lost loved ones. As I listen, sometimes I want to ask, what is the real question? The real question has to do with guilt and loss, and people want to know how to get on with their lives.

One of the things I hope my books do is to cause people to ask themselves: Why am I here on this earth? What is my purpose? What is my purpose now, especially in view of the death of someone I deeply love?

No amount of grief will bring the person back. No amount of pleading with God will change the spiritual destination of that loved one. What can happen is to make that loss the foundation for reaching out to others. Support groups, for example, can be a great energizer and a source of encouragement.

I've also met people who have joined suicide-prevention groups and they tell me they're determined to become more sensitive to the people around them and to look for the signals. They've done research on suicide and potential suicide victims.

"I can spot those who are ready to cash in on life," one man said. "Maybe it's because I've been involved so much in suicide prevention. It's like a warning bell rings around certain people. I know. I can't explain, but when I talk to them, *I just know*."

He was one of those individuals who has worked his way out of a "bungled suicide attempt" (his words) through a dark valley of grief because of the loss of his wife in a traffic accident that he caused. He came through it and has found a reason for living. "My reason for living is so that I can stop others from doing what I tried to do when I wanted to end my life."

Too few of us stop and ponder the question: Why am I here? What is my purpose? We may never have a complete answer, but I do know that as we seek the answer and as we gain more understanding, we have peace. We find our *raison d'être*.

I can't give people the reason, because that must come from their own self-discovery and self-awareness, but the one thing I can say is this, "You are here because God wants you here. Because he wants you here, you have a reason to live."

Your life is precious to God. He alone is the giver of life; he alone is entitled to end our earthly existence.

Lord of my life, remind me that I'm here and I'm alive because you have created me and you have given me a purpose for remaining on this earth. Help me discover my purpose as my days on Earth dwindle and I draw closer to you. Amen.

And I heard a voice from heaven saying, "Write this down:
Blessed are those who die in the Lord from now on.
Yes, says the Spirit, they are blessed indeed,
for they will rest from all their toils and trials . . ."

—REVELATION 14:13[*]

89

"THEY DON'T MISS ME"

"The most important message I've received from *90 Minutes in Heaven*," wrote one man, "is that you've helped me to realize how joyful people are in heaven."

Another person wrote of how contented people are in heaven, and was glad that they don't miss us. She wrote that she missed the people in her life who had died but she knew her grief would disappear when she had her reunion with them.

By contrast, at one book signing a woman leaned over and whispered that she wished she could communicate with her late husband. "I miss him so much."

"What would you communicate to him?" I asked softly. "Would you say, 'I miss you' 'I'm sorry you died' 'It hurt me that you got sick'? All the things that you'd like to tell him involve sad or painful things for him to hear. Why would you want to communicate that to him in heaven? Would he be able to feel better if he knew you grieved for him? If he knew you were sad?"

"No, I wouldn't want to say that—"

I smiled at the woman and asked, "Even if you could send the message, it wouldn't get there."

When she looked surprised, I said, "Heaven is a place of total happiness and peace. Nothing—absolutely nothing—can destroy that perfection. The message would be discarded and God would never allow it to arrive. It's as if there is a barrier between our sadness, loss, tears, and disease and the flawlessness inside heaven's gates. The sad things are on this side, but they're not in heaven."

Part of the message of hope I bring is that we can focus on preparing ourselves for the joy, the bliss, and the perfection of heaven.

Of course, those of us still on earth miss our loved ones. They were vital parts of our lives. They cared about us and loved us. To lose an important person is sad. But there is no sadness in heaven.

One woman with tears in her eyes said, "You don't know what comfort this brings to me. My husband is there—enjoying his new, healthy life. He has no pain. His long battle with cancer is over and he's perfectly well and healthy." She wiped away a few tears and said, "And what brings me even more comfort is that he'll be at the gate of heaven at the head of my welcome committee."

"Yes. He will be there. And he'll be smiling because he's perfectly and totally happy."

Loving God, sometimes I miss those I've lost. I yearn to talk to them, to share my pain and my heartaches and even to rejoice in my victories. But even to tell of victories involves my having to talk about overcoming obstacles. Thank you for reminding me that those in heaven are beyond sadness and live in total bliss. And one day I can join them in that celebration. Thank you. Amen.

*Therefore, since we are surrounded by such a huge crowd
of witnesses to the life of faith, let us strip off
every weight that slows us down, especially the sin
that so easily hinders our progress.*

—HEBREWS 12:1*

90

SEE YOU AT THE GATE

One of the experiences that I marvel over most about my brief trip to heaven was the people who met me at the gate. I saw my grandfather and a crowd of people, some of whom didn't know each other on earth. But I saw each of those individuals who had impacted my life and helped me on my personal journey to heaven.

When I speak, I sometimes say, "Before I went to heaven, I wondered if my loved ones who had died knew what was going on here with me? The answer is no, they don't. Did they know I was coming? Yes, they knew—trust me, they knew. They don't sit around on the porch and wait for us to show up, but they know."

They were there to greet me because they helped me to get there. A lot of other people waited for me inside the gate, people with whom I would have fellowship. But those who stood at the gate were the special ones, the individuals who impacted my life and prepared me for my journey heavenward.

One of the joys that is often misunderstood or neglected is that none of those who greeted me in heaven talked about those who weren't yet there. They didn't focus on that aspect or wonder when the loved one would come. Heaven is free from time restraints, so a few years of waiting are like nothing.

Heaven is a place of total celebration and where we meet all the saints from the beginning of time. They include Peter, Paul, David, Sarah, Samuel, Rahab, and Hannah. They include the unnamed people in the Bible such as the woman at the well or the slave girl who told the king of Syria about the prophet Elisha, or the four men who lowered their paralyzed friend through the roof so Jesus could heal him.

When we get to heaven we'll meet all those people who played incredible roles in history and we'll also meet those who played insignificant roles.

I confess that my thoughts often go back to the gate and I think about the people who will meet me there. They are the true heroes of my life. They are the ones who obeyed God and opened the way for me to enter heaven and helped me make my personal reservation.

Sometimes it's good for us to pause and think about the

people who made the trip easier for us. We owe them so much. What would it be like if we thought of them as our cheering section? What if we thought of them as special messengers in our lives here on earth whose task is to prepare us for our special place in heaven? Most of the people I saw weren't aware of what they had done for me on earth. They didn't do the loving acts so they could be there to embrace me and rejoice at being part of my entourage, but they did the natural thing: They shared of themselves and helped me to make heaven a certainty.

If heaven is our destination, we will have our own cheering section to welcome us to the place of never-ending joy. They may be pastors or Sunday school teachers, loving parents, a compassionate neighbor, or praying coworkers.

This might also be a good time for us to think about those whom *we* will one day meet at the gate. For whom have we cared enough to invite them to follow Jesus Christ? To whom have we demonstrated the power and peace of the Lord? For whose salvation have we prayed? Some of those we welcome may be those that we unconsciously touched. Perhaps we encouraged them simply by living a godly life around them. Maybe there are those yet to leave this life who may be waiting for us to help them find the path of righteousness. It's not too late to become part of many cheering sections when others reach the gate.

Not only will we have people at the gate waiting for us—but

one day we can be part of the welcoming committee for those who follow because of us.

God, sometimes I feel as if I do so little to usher others into the kingdom. Remind me that being your witness and helper is more than praying with sinners as they open up to you. It's also praying for you to open their hearts. It's living a life that reflects Jesus Christ around others. Thanks, God, that I will be welcomed. I love to focus on the reality that I can be part of many welcoming committees. Thank you, Lord. Amen.